AMERICAN INDIANS TODAY

AMERICAN INDIANS TODAY

Olga Hoyt

Illustrated with photographs

Abelard-Schuman

New York

Manufactured in the United States of America

Library of Congress Cataloging in Publication Data
Hoyt, Olga.
    American Indians today.
    SUMMARY: Describes the modern way of life of over
200 Indian tribes in the United States, including their
efforts to obtain equal rights and increased
government aid.
    Bibliography: p.
    1. Indians of North America—Juvenile literature.
[1. Indians of North America] I. Title.
E77.4.H6   970.1   79–141865
ISBN 0–200–71891–6

4   5   6   7   8   9   10

*To the American Indians—
may they realize their hopes for the future*

CONTENTS

8

LIST OF
ILLUSTRATIONS

10

PREFACE

The American Indian has been largely a forgotten person by the general public for hundreds of years. Now that Indians are speaking out, and the government is becoming more concerned not only with their rights but their living conditions and their futures, it seems timely to take a look at how many of the Indians live today.

In this book I have attempted to give a sampling of some of the Indian conditions in the United States. For my information I relied heavily on material supplied by tribal leaders and bureau officials who work with the various tribes. I queried over 200 tribes and I am grateful for the cooperative responses I received from hundreds of Indians. I was fortunate enough also to visit a number of reservations in the summer of 1971.

I did not touch on the Indians in Alaska, for they are a book in themselves.

It is to be hoped that this book proves enlightening reading to those who have not been acquainted with the American Indian today.

Olga G. Hoyt
Chartwell
Severna Park, Maryland
January, 1972

1

INDIAN PROBLEMS

There are many problems facing the Indian tribes in America today, and because the Indians themselves have become more vocal about the injustices done by the white man in the past, and now show more public determination to solve their own problems, there is real hope for the first time that this minority will progress toward sharing the benefits and well-being of most Americans.

The exploits of famed Indian fighters, such as Sitting Bull and Geronimo, are so well known as to be parodies of the Indian peoples. These men resisted the white encroachment of their territory many years ago, and we are all familiar with the tales. But until recently few Americans recognized the fact that the Indians of today, like other minority groups, are working within their tribes not only to right the wrongs of the past, but to build new strength and prosperity for themselves.

Dramatic moves have been made by the Indians to call attention to their very existence in a country that is beset by war, black-white racial strife, and youthful rebellion. One of the significant Indian displays was the landing on Alcatraz toward the end of 1969—the Indians came not as conquerors, but to rally public feeling for the problems and hopes of all Indians. On Alcatraz Island, a bleak, decaying twelve-acre rock in San Francisco Bay, was an old prison fortress. The Indians spectacularly took over the old ruined Spanish buildings, where green moss and wild vines flourished. They claimed the island "by right of discovery," and they proposed to make Alcatraz an Indian center, planned and operated by the Indian people. This move was a gesture to focus attention on the Indians, their problems and their future. It succeeded very well, although the Indians later lost the right to occupy the island.

Vine Deloria, Jr., one of the most eloquent Indian (a Standing Rock Sioux) spokesmen, and a talented author and law student, urged the Indians to leave their past glories to the ministrations of the historians, and to embark on an aggressive program of rebuilding the tribes. And that is just what the Indians in America are trying to do today. They are by no means on the warpath in the manner of the black revolutionaries; however, they are determined to call the white man's attention to their problems, and they intend to do it nonviolently.

The Indians throughout the last century have lost much of their land to the white man, by treaties and trickery. The loss of this land has hindered the economic development of many of the tribes. In recent years tribal leaders have become vocal about this loss of land, and their efforts to call public and government attention to this particular problem are beginning to get results. Some months ago, President Richard Nixon signed a bill which restored to the Taos Pueblo Indians of New

Mexico the use of 48,000 acres in the Carson National Forest. This tract had played a role in the tribe's religion ever since the fourteenth century. It had been appropriated by an uncaring federal government in 1906 for the creation of a national forest. Because of their persistent and noisy efforts, the Taos Pueblo Indians were given the right to use the land for religious ceremonies, hunting, fishing, and forage for livestock. When the President signed the bill, he proclaimed that "paternalism" was now of the past.

"Paternalism," the taking care of the Indians, has long been the policy of the government toward the various Indian tribes, but as the Taos Pueblo story shows, this policy—largely because of the growing strength of many of the Indian tribes—is being replaced by a policy of self-determination. For too long the Indians have been abused, ignored, mollified by token aid, or taken care of; now there appears to be an effort by the government to treat them as dignified people who can—with help—direct their own futures.

Various tribes throughout the country have been—and are — faced by vicious problems: they are poor, they are sick, they haven't enough land, or good land, they get inferior education, they are isolated, they are discriminated against, they suffer rashes of juvenile delinquency, and alcoholism.

Each tribe in the country is unique. Each has its own successes and failures. In America, over 660,000 persons are classified as Indians today, and there are over 250 tribes. There are many Indians off the reservations, in the cities, or wherever they can find a livelihood. Just as one cannot describe the conditions of one Indian tribe as "typical" of all tribes, one cannot paint one portrait of "the American Indian."

It is a good idea to listen to what the Indians themselves say on the subject. The Navajo tribal chairman, Peter MacDonald, recently reported:

> Over the years, the native Americans have been subject to public scrutiny in books, newspapers, magazines, movies, television, etc., but yet the real nature of our people is still misunderstood and their motives often misrepresented or misinterpreted.
>
> The native Americans are human. As such they have the same basic needs as any other group of humanity—the same spiritual, economical, and social needs. As people, they have differences as there are over 200 tribes in this country, each with its own language, culture and customs. As individuals, they have individuality just like any human. Some are easy going, others are temperamental, and some talkative, some quiet, some aggressive, others passive, some creative, others conformists, etc., just like any other individual anywhere.
>
> Therefore, to include these various tribes, or even any tribe, under one label or characteristic is to do them an injustice. Most young native Americans are interested in their heritage and wish to be treated on an equal basis with all other people. To write about these people, the writer should keep in mind their pride, their right to be treated as human beings, and not just as objects to be studied.

It is obvious that no white—nor any one Indian—can speak of Indian problems or conditions, or hopes, or plans, or successes, or failures, but only of specific circumstances of specific Indians.

A sampling of the conditions of a number of Indian tribes in the United States is instructive in learning how certain Indians live today.

2

THE INDIANS AND THE GOVERNMENT

The Indians have lived in America for thousands of years, the white man for less than 500 years. The ancestors of the Indians probably came to this continent between 10,000 and 20,000 years ago. They settled from one shore to another—the Spaniards found them in Florida and in California, when they arrived in the New World. After the white man arrived on the East Coast, many Indians found themselves harassed and pushed westward by the newcomers—settlers who were ever expanding their territorial control. Fighting, cholera, smallpox, the intrusion of fur trappers, the rush to the gold fields, the granting of railroad rights-of-way—all these took their toll of Indian lives and Indian land.

In the early days of white–Indian relations, the federal government which had been organized to form the United States of America signed treaties with individual Indian tribes. The Delaware Treaty of 1778 is the earliest such treaty. It spoke of "peace and friendship" which was necessary between the peoples of the United States and the tribe.

The various Indian tribes were treated as sovereign, yet dependent, domestic nations. The federal government had to deal with these nations if they wanted special land concessions, and when land concessions were made according to various treaties, the government assumed the responsibility to protect the lands that the tribes reserved for their own use against the encroachment of United States citizens. Thus early treaties were made, establishing certain reservations for certain Indian tribes. There was, for example, the Treaty of Medicine Creek of 1854, which established some of the reservations in Washington, depriving the Indians of much land. In 1868, after numerous military–Indian skirmishes, a treaty was concluded by the federal government with the Navajo tribe which established a Navajo reservation. Such was the pattern throughout the country; after conflict and strife, treaties were signed with the Indians granting them the use of specific land for their purposes. It must be remembered, however, that the land was not *given* to the Indians, who usually owned it anyway, but held "in trust" by the federal government for the Indians and Indian uses.

Then in 1871, the government decided, through Congress, that it would sign no more treaties with tribes. The Dawes Act of 1887 was called the Allotment Act, and it, in effect, divided the existing reservations into allotments of 160 acres each; each Indian was given an allotment for farming. The rest of the reservation was considered surplus and could be settled by non-Indians. What a sorry day that was for the Indians! Pressured and pushed and pulled, many of the Indians were not able to resist the whites and some sold their lands for as little as a bottle of whiskey. The lands belonging to the Indians, therefore, shrank drastically in total size.

As the years passed after allotment, it became evident that by such a program the government had cast the majority of Indians into poverty, since they no longer had a sufficient land base for living. In 1926, a thorough study was made (the Meriam report), which concluded that the allotment system was a failure as far as the Indian was concerned. It has been estimated that by 1934, over 90 million acres of land were lost to the Indians—in reality—stolen from them.

As a result of the Meriam report, allotment was stopped in 1934 by the Indian Reorganization Act, which was a basic charter of Indian rights. Tribes were given status as federal corporations, and efforts were made, through government help, to build up the Indian lands that had suffered encroachment in the past.

Government help had been provided for the Indians early in the nineteenth century by the establishment of the Bureau of Indian Affairs. The policies of the Bureau, issued from the Department of Interior, went through many changes throughout the years, and inspired much controversy and dislike, among Indians and non-Indians. Even today, although the Bureau members are dedicated to assisting the Indians, there is dissatisfaction in many quarters with their attitudes and accomplishments. Dissatisfaction is probably a mild word. There have been charges of "colonialism" and "paternalism." One recently published book, prepared by the Citizens' Advocate Center, *Our Brother's Keeper: The Indian in White America,* is a diatribe against the Bureau, depicting it as "our Brother's Keeper," reaching into *every* aspect of the Indians' individual and communal lives.

As recently as September, 1971, twenty-six Indians were arrested after occupying two rooms in Washington's BIA building when they came to protest "gross misconduct and criminal injustice" by some BIA officials.

This is strong criticism of the Bureau, and similar feeling is widespread. But, as Vine Deloria, Jr., has said, "There are good men in the Bureau who want to do good, who want to do the right thing." However, ". . . the right thing for many people who want to do good is always in terms of their own value system. God help us from those who want to help us!"

These views are held by many Indians because they have found, through the years, that a great number of persons in the government bureaucracy are authoritarian. Harrison Loesch, Assistant Secretary of the Interior, noted this when he spoke early in 1972 of the "love-hate" relationship between the American Indian and those in the BIA who consider him their ward. These officials talk about what should be done *for* the Indians, what direction planning *for* the Indians should take. To offset this attitude, and this charge, many of today's Bureau officials are publicly insistent about a new role: one of guidance. The new Bureau officials write indignantly that they prepare no projects *for* the Indians. The Indians make the plans, they say, and the Bureau assists them with financial and technical aid.

Thus, one big problem facing many Indians is how to be ready to assume greater leadership in planning for Indian lives. They *have* been dependent on the government in the past. Today they are striving to become independent tribes, with Indian leaders, working for and with their own people.

Though many tribal leaders resent past dependency on the government, by the same token, most do not wish to sever their ties completely. The Indians always had, after the conclusion of treaties in the nineteenth century, a special relationship with the federal government, as in lands held "in trust," and federal responsibility for administering the affairs of the individual Indian tribes. Under this relationship the tribes were able, after allotment stopped, to regain land for their communities until progress was halted by World War II, when such domestic spending was suspended. Then, in the 1950's, instead of a resurgence of cooperation between Indians and the federal government, came what was to be known as the "termination" policy. Termination simply meant severing that special trusteeship between tribes and the federal government. The move was started in Congress by some individuals who thought they had the proper solution to the Indian problem. Charges were made that the reservations were the "havens of irresponsibility," and that the federal government had been too protective of Indian rights.

Termination of federal supervision was disastrous to a number of tribes. One outstanding example of the deleterious effect of termination was what happened to the Menominee Indian tribe in Wisconsin. They owned a forest and a tribal sawmill. The business was operated primarily to give employment to the members of the tribe, though often it showed a profit. It was, because of the special relationship with the federal government, exempt from corporate taxation. The tribe spent most of the income from the sawmill on services for the members of the tribe. They had their own hospital, and provided for their own law enforcement on the reservation. With the termination of federal supervision, the sawmill was no longer tax exempt—as a matter of fact, the government immediately presented a tax bill of 55 percent of the year's profits. So, a vicious circle started. To pay the bill, the mill had to become more automated. The more automated the mill became, the more tribal members were left without jobs. Without jobs, unemployment rose. To take care of these unemployed the county taxed the sawmill. Today the tribe is still recovering from that blow.

The policy of termination was also disastrous because of the apprehension it created among many Indian tribes. Some tribes hesitated to consider new programs, fearing that termination would wipe out any progress they made. Though years have passed since the termination era, even today various Indian tribes are distrustful of both the Bureau and the termination theory—in spite of the fact that both Presidents Lyndon B. Johnson and Richard Nixon have publicly assured the Indians and the nation that the goal for the Indians is self-help.

President Nixon's views on the Indians received full notice during his campaign for President in the fall of 1968: "The special responsibilities of the federal government to the Indian people will be acknowledged."

By midsummer of 1971, it became apparent to the general public that policies toward the Indians *were* changing. The Indians had voiced their desires to plan for their own futures. Their distaste for what they considered to be the manipulation of their programs and their lives was obvious. President Nixon sent a message to Congress about the Indians that made front-page headlines. The President denounced the "centuries of injustice" to the American Indians. He repudiated the policy that had been official for seventeen years—that of termination. He proposed a program that would enable the Indians to take over the operation of federal programs, which he admitted had "frequently proven to be ineffective and demeaning." The Indians were to be given the chance to do the planning for and administering of their own future. What a change in climate had come about in a period of 100 years!

Nevertheless the American Indians are still the "most deprived and most isolated minority group in our nation," as President Nixon termed them. How some of them live and plan and hope today will be described in the following chapters.

3

THE NAVAJO INDIANS

The greatest concentration of Indians today is on reservations in the western part of the United States. The Navajo Indians are by far the largest tribe in the country with 130,000 members scattered over 16 million acres of northern Arizona, southern Utah and western New Mexico.

Navajos have been in their country for a long time. Even by the early 1600's, they were considered an aggressive and powerful tribe; they acquired horses and sheep from the Spaniards, and also a knowledge of metal and woodworking. For centuries they were left undisturbed; it was not until 1846 that a United States military expedition went into the Navajo territory and conflict began. After years of fighting, an effective treaty with the Navajo tribe, establishing a reservation, was signed in 1868. Through the years, the size of that reservation was increased (unlike the situation on many other reservations where the land area was markedly decreased), until by 1934 the land area approximated the size of the reservation as it is.

Navajo leaders inspect land for further development, Angel Peak Recreation Area, San Juan County, New Mexico

Today the Navajos are among the leaders of the Indians seeking a new role in American affairs. The tribal chairman is young, energetic Peter MacDonald. Previously, he was the head of the Office of Navajo Economic Opportunity, an important and effective organization, and now he promises much for his people, as stated in his inaugural address in 1971:

First, what is rightfully ours, we must protect. What is rightfully due us, we must claim. Second, what we depend on from others we must replace with the labor of our own hands and the skills of our own people.

Third, what we do not have we must bring into being. We must create for ourselves. . . .

We are owed special federal funds for education, manpower, highway construction, economic development, vocational education and for other purposes. We are due a share of these as Navajos and as citizens. These federal funds are ours by right and by law. We must claim them.

Right now we depend on much from others that we must begin to provide for ourselves. We are forced to depend on others to run our schools, build our roads, administer our health programs, construct our houses, manage our industries, sell us cars, cash our checks and operate our trading posts. This must cease.

These were strong words. Mark well that Peter MacDonald is a strong man who provides powerful leadership for the Navajo. The tribe has assets of $200 million available to build a growing Navajo nation. What Peter MacDonald was saying is what many Indian leaders have been saying: the Indians must and will plan for *their own* future. They will do so within the framework of the tribal government, which is today responsible

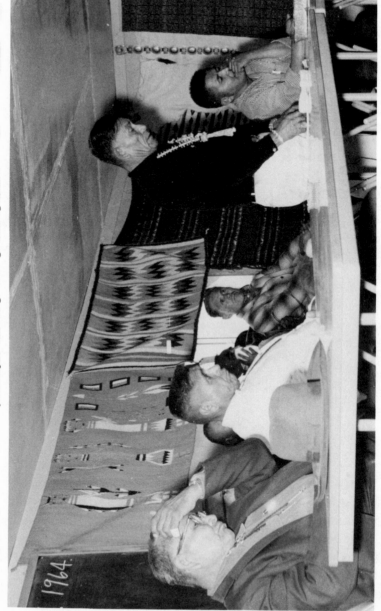

Navajo Chapter Meeting, local governing board

to the federal government, to the Secretary of the Interior, and the Bureau of Indian Affairs.

This Navajo tribal government is responsive to the wishes of its peoples as expressed at local meetings. The Navajo leaders are *of* the people, and responsible *to* the people for trying to solve the many special problems of the Navajos.

One cannot possibly describe "a Navajo," or "a Navajo" way of life. The reservation encompasses such a vast area that there are tremendous differences in the land, in housing, in education, in employment, in health, and in retention of the old culture. The people range from among the most educated of all Indians, according to national standards, to the most illiterate (40,000 Navajos are functionally illiterate in English). There are signs of the modern, and signs of the old. There are Navajo Boy Scouts, and Navajo PTA—bingo games, rodeos, and basketball tournaments, and also Indian dances and powwows. And Navajo women still spin and dye wool for rugs. The nation has lonely sheepherders, and men in Vietnam.

Sometimes the land is forbidding—vast sweeps and flat semiarid mesas and canyons, unfenced plain, with a winter climate that can be bitterly cold after sundown. The family units are scattered over a wide area, linked to one another and to shopping, health and education facilities by a series of rocky, dirt roads, some of them impassable in severe weather. On such inhospitable land, many a family lives in a hogan, a six- or eight-sided, log and mud dwelling with a dirt floor, and a central smoke hole in the roof.

The cooking is done over an open fire on a stove made from a gasoline drum. To secure water, a family may have to haul it by wagon or pickup truck. Sometimes, for a family living in an isolated area, the nearest spring may be ten miles away. Most

An isolated Navajo hogan and sheep

of the people who live in hogans in remote areas do not speak English. They earn their living by raising sheep, weaving rugs, or working silver. As one drives through the main roads of the reservation, one is struck by the bleakness, by the obvious poverty and hardship that must prevail for these Indians. Yet these people live vastly different lives from those Navajos who live in the towns such as Window Rock, Shiprock and Many Farms. There, in close communities, are three- and four-bed-room modern houses with landscaped grounds.

Many of the facts about the Navajo life are shocking. For example, while less than 10 percent of the United States popula-tion lives below the "poverty line," among the Navajos, 90 percent are below that line. And while 3 to 7 percent of the United States population was unemployed in 1971, 70 percent of the Navajos were unemployed.

The infant mortality rate among the Navajos is twice the national one, and it can largely be traced to malnutrition. There is still real hunger in the rural areas of the reservation. Now, people in these rural areas are often worse off as far as diet is concerned than they were in their grandparents' time. Then food was raised at home, and goats provided milk and meat. There were sheep to provide meat and clothing. There were garden plots which provided fresh vegetables. There was little need for money because the Navajos traded for what they could not raise. Today, the population has increased greatly and the land available to each family is less; water supplies are more limited, and it is estimated that about a third of the water is brackish and unusable. The people are no longer self-sustaining.

Another problem is the distribution of food supplies. Fresh fruit and vegetables, eggs, milk, cheese and fish are rarely avail-able at the trading posts and, when they are, the prices are so high as to keep the poor people from buying them. And even if the Navajo families get these foods, often there is no way to keep them fresh, because most Navajos have no electricity, gas, or water service.

In order to combat many of these problems, the Office of Navajo Economic Opportunity was established by the tribal council in 1965 as "the command post for the Navajo War on Poverty." It started at the local level, forming a program for community development, hoping that local people would be stimulated to improve their communities. It has tried to help the 5,000–10,000 migrant workers, to better the conditions under which they work, and to give them improved housing, medical care, education and higher wages. ONEO also has attacked the number one health problem of the Navajo Nation —alcoholism—with a program of community alcoholism treatment and education. Since ONEO began the program, it has assisted almost 1,000 members who sought aid. The cure rate was amazing—more than 50 percent. However, this program for alcoholics is still sadly lacking the funds and hospital facilities to service the estimated 10,000 Navajos who need help.

Other programs of the ONEO include the Vista program, a home improvement training program, which gives the men construction skills, so that the substandard and unsanitary living conditions for many families can be improved.

A neighborhood Youth Corps Program provides paid work experience and intensive counseling for both in-school youth and dropouts. Head Start is operating 92 classrooms, serving almost 2,000 preschoolers. DNA (Dinebeiina Nahiilna Be Agaditahe, Inc.), the legal aid service, is a part of the ONEO and has served over 6,000 tribal members, with a staff of ten practicing attorneys.

At the same time that the ONEO is trying to better conditions for individual Indians, the tribal leaders are trying to develop the reservation so that there will be more jobs and higher incomes. They have established an industrial park with funds provided by the federal government (through the Economic Development Administration). Here, for example, is a factory to manufacture low-cost homes. These houses are great innovations for the Navajos, for they are module homes that can be delivered to the site, ready for occupancy, complete with all electrical wiring, plumbing, bathroom fixtures, kitchen cabinets, exterior and interior walls, floor coverings and roofing.

This plant is next to one owned by General Dynamics, a huge industrial combine. General Dynamics has been so pleased with its operation on the reservation, that it recently ran a two-page advertisement in a popular national magazine praising the Navajos:

> . . . the Navajo.
> His roots are set deep in the land he fought for, lost and regained over 100 years ago . . . he has set up his own government, established tribally owned industries and a ten-million-dollar college scholarship fund.
> He knows the natural resources he has relied on will eventually run out. To avoid the economic disaster that would follow, the Navajo is drawing on his greatest resources: the Navajo.
> He's bringing outside industry to his reservation by offering a pool of fast-learning people whose natural intelligence exceeds their formal education. . . .
> In our facility . . . they're putting together highly complex electronic assemblies for aerospace systems and tear-

Maria Martinez and her famous pottery

ing apart a lot of popular misconceptions about Indians in
general and Navajos in particular.

By building a new economy, the Navajo is making one
thing clear . . . he's not about to be counted as a "vanishing
American."

Other corporation-owned factories are coming to the reservation too, and many Indians have secured employment there.
Other Navajos work for schools, hospitals, in water development and road building. They handle all tribal, government and
state operations on tribal land. Most of those who work off the
reservation go to nearby cities, but often they go as far away as
Illinois and California. Other Navajos have seasonal employment in Idaho, Colorado and nearby states as agricultural
workers.

Farming, of course, has been practiced by the Navajos from
the very beginning of the tribe's history. Since much of the
reservation land is harsh and dry, farms are usually confined to
areas where the soil yields good crops. Fine vegetables and
fruits are displayed at the Navajo fairs held each year in Shiprock, Window Rock and Tuba City, in Arizona.

As with many other southwestern Indian tribes, the Navajos
are excellent craftsmen; the best-known Navajo crafts are weaving and silversmithing. These crafts are practiced in the homes
or in shops on and off the reservation, along with some basketry
and pottery making. The rugs and other woven goods are col-
lected each year by stores, as far away as New York; the same
is true of silver items and paintings.

Schools are scattered all over the reservation. There are
boarding schools and day schools, to which pupils travel by bus.
Some of the schools are run by the federal government; others

Smoke Signal School on Navajo Reservation in Chinle, Arizona

are self-operated. The percentage of attendance is high. The
Navajos want to better the education of their children, and to
extend it. That is why, late in 1969, they formed an association
called *Dine Biolta*— the people's schools. The major aim of the
group is to have the Navajo people run their own good schools.
The members of the association want not only Navajo control
of the schools on the reservation, but they also want those
schools to offer bilingual-bicultural studies. As one school principal said, "Not much learning takes place when the teachers
talk to children as if the children have always spoken English.
Why not teach them in their own language? The child thinks
in Navajo." For this, many more Navajo teachers are needed.

In spite of the Navajo plea for more education in Navajo
ways, one Bureau of Indian Affairs official said he felt that
much of the tribal culture definitely has been retained in the
tribe. Most Navajos, including many of school age, speak their
own tongue as well as English.

It is indeed true that the culture of the Navajos is not lost.
Take religion: there are many established churches on the reservation and in nearby cities, and also many independent missionaries, yet the Navajos also still practice and believe in their own
religion.

In the field of health, many of the old tribal beliefs are still
current. The medicine man not only exists, he is very powerful
in tribal affairs. The Navajo feels that illness represents man's
disharmony with nature and that only the medicine man can
correct the disharmony. Health occupies a very important position in the Navajo religion, and the healers or medicine men are
also spiritual leaders of the tribe.

In everyday living, one out of seven of the older Navajos
continues to practice Indian medicine to drive out evil spirits,

thus posing difficulties for modern doctors and Public Health Service personnel in getting the Navajos to accept and use the non-Indian practical knowledge, without undermining their faith. One Public Health Service official said that, "the physicians who have contact with the Indians could do much if they knew some of the fundamentals of the Indians' outlook and religion."

In spite of such difficulties of bringing modern medicine to the Navajos, the health of the tribe as a whole has improved, so that tuberculosis and infant diseases—the old killers—are no longer as prevalent as in the past.

The Public Health Service maintains well-staffed hospitals in the larger communities, and clinics in many of the smaller ones. Their nurses travel from one small community to another at regular times, yet there is still much to be done in raising health standards.

There is much to be done everywhere on the reservation, but it *can* be done, as Peter MacDonald told a group of students:

> We can be a great nation. There are enough strong people to make it so. We have young, imaginative and educated leaders who can pull all the loose ends together for a great future for all. . . . We need to . . . draw on the strengths we have inherited to move forward as one people, united and unbeatable.

4

THE INDIANS
OF ARIZONA

Many American Indian tribes feel caught between two worlds, their Indian tribal world with its special beliefs and customs, and the modern world of the white man. This conflict, or adjustment, between the two climates is often mentioned by tribal leaders; it cannot help but be paramount for many tribes who have lived peacefully for generations as farmers, or shepherds, or cattlemen. But the more complex society becomes, the more it is apparent that the old ways are not enough to bring a solid economy, good health, good education and material well-being to some of the tribes.

The Hopis are an excellent example of a people struggling, and generally succeeding, to adjust to a new society, while not losing their individuality. It must be remembered that most Indians do not want to be *assimilated* into a white society. They want to remain Indians, with an Indian culture. This is especially true with the Hopis.

They are a very conservative and religious people who have

retained their culture, for more than a thousand years, living on three adjoining mesas high above the northern Arizona desert, within the Navajo reservation. Their reservation, a rectangular piece of land of about one and a half million acres, was set up by presidential executive order in 1882. They are an island of 6,000 Hopis surrounded by many thousands of Navajos. Though known as "the peaceful people," (the meaning of Hopi), through the years they have had disputes with their Navajo neighbors over the ownership of land. A settlement was finally made in 1962 by an Arizona district court, but even today, further court action is being sought to evict certain Navajo families from what is considered Hopi land.

The Hopis traditionally have grown corn, vegetables and fruits on the desert lands at the foot of their mesas. They are among the very best of the world's dry farmers, as well as competent shepherds and cattlemen. Many of the Indians have developed manual skills such as carpentry, mechanics and modern masonry, which complement their own excellent skills in the arts and crafts. Their pottery, basketry, weaving, carving and silversmithing are, and always have been, a very important part of their tribal economy.

But today there is evidence that the Hopis are accepting and adopting many of the ways of non-Indian culture, in order to develop the reservation. The tribal leaders have initiated projects, which, with the aid of the government through the Bureau of Indian Affairs, have helped their economy immeasurably. The Hopis' tribal cultural center is a $900,000 tourism complex. It includes a thirty-three unit motel, a restaurant, a museum and a gift-craft shop, all of which not only provide income, but employment for Hopis. The tribe itself has invested over $1½ million in a factory on tribal land, which employs over 200 Indians. Recently, a new Hopi Headquarters was opened at Oraibi; it was built with tribal funds and entirely with tribal labor. Homes are being constructed on a mutual help plan, by which labor contributes toward ownership. These houses have three bedrooms, a complete kitchen and air conditioning.

The tribe is now receiving large orders for its woodworking, which furnishes the U.S. government with desk letter boxes, coat racks, display racks, blackboards, and its construction aprons and cotton bags.

In spite of all this activity on the reservation, living conditions are still not ideal. Many of the Indians retain the old culture and are unwilling to accept the modern ways. As a tribal spokesman said, "Some of the Indian people have no desire to change their way of life. These people, known locally as traditionalists, are, by non-Indian standards, living in poverty, but their wishes to remain in the present condition are respected by the tribe."

So, although the progressive members of the Hopi tribe realize that they cannot better their own conditions without adapting the industrial know-how of the white society, there are still those who live and want to live the way Hopis always have, untouched by progress.

Among other tribes in Arizona, which feel the strain and conflict of incorporating the old culture into a new economy, are the Apaches. Apaches as a people are perhaps better known than many Indian tribes, since they were such fierce fighters. In the beginning, the Apaches were mostly wanderers, and raiders of both white settlers and other Indians. They had a well-deserved reputation for their warlike disposition, and there were many battles and massacres. Perhaps the most famous were the exploits of Geronimo, who finally surrendered with his band in 1886. Some years before, in 1871, President Ulysses S. Grant established the White Mountain Reservation. On this reservation were settled the two tribes of Apaches: the White Mountain Apaches, and the San Carlos Apaches. Eventually the reservation was split in two, with each group receiving between 1.6 million and 1.8 million acres of some of the most beautiful land in eastern Arizona.

These Apaches were, and still are, very proud of their heritage, and though they have made great strides in adjusting to the white man's culture, some of them are reluctant to accept the new ways.

The San Carlos Reservation—where about 4,700 Indians live—had to be moved after its creation because of the construction of the Coolidge Dam. The reservation has long been a fine cattle-raising area, and today this cattle industry is big business with annual sales in the millions of dollars.

Conditions on the reservation for the Apaches have changed drastically. In previous years these Indians lived in old brush and canvas huts, today most of them live in frame houses. Where once they existed on a limited diet of pinto beans, tortillas and fried bread, with beef or bacon, potatoes, melons, squash and Indian corn when available, today their meals are generally much the same as those of the non-Indians. Tribally owned stores on the reservation carry fresh fruits, vegetables, meats and other foods found in most other grocery stores of the same size. Teen-agers and many of the older Indians wear modern dress, with the men preferring blue jeans, brightly colored shirts, cowboy boots and wide-brimmed hats, although many of the older women wear more traditional clothes. Travel is mainly by pickup truck,

San Carlos Apache wickiup, Arizona

credit: Arthur Sirdofsky

and horses are used only for the rodeos and in the cattle operations.

Over the years, the ways of the white man's society have reached these Apaches, and yet as a group they are low on the economic scale and conditions are hard for many. Income is low, and unemployment is about 40 percent of the available work force. The educational level is also low—ninth-grade level —in spite of the fact that there is a school on the reservation for the younger children and the older ones attend the public schools in Globe. There is a hospital nearby, operated by the Public Health Service, and there are two trading posts on the reservation. Housing development has been slow, but recently a contract was made for sixty-eight new homes, which would finish a 150-home plan for the reservation. Timber is being harvested, and a road construction program is under way to develop the Geronimo Trail, which it is hoped will attract tourists to the reservation.

It is perhaps the land which holds the greatest potential for the economic betterment of the San Carlos Apaches. The reservation consists of much beautiful and untouched land. It ranges from high mountain country, with blue spruce, pine and aspens, mountain lakes and trout streams, wild flowers and high green meadows, to rolling cedar country, to rock formations and sunny desert highlands. The tribe has become aware of the promises of the land, and they now offer hunting rights in primitive areas for deer, elk, bear and javalina (wild pig), as well as fishing, sight-seeing at Indian ruins, and general recreation. The tribal leaders are planning to take further advantage of their land, with two major tourist projects under way, one at Senewca Lake, and the other at San Carlos Lake. But here, too, the Indians realize that they really cannot develop a sound economy unless they bring industry onto the reservation. Thus they are planning for the construction of an industrial park, which should bring the jobs that are so badly needed.

The White Mountain Apaches live on the neighboring Fort Apache Reservation. And for these Apaches, too, there is the struggle between the old and the new. Perhaps this struggle is even more pronounced here because the White Mountain Apaches have retained, to a greater extent than many other tribes, their own culture. Through their language, dress, ceremonies and rites, traditional stories, songs, social customs, and distinctive behavior patterns and tribal values, they have kept a great deal of the past. The problem of adjusting the old to the new is persistent. Recently the tribal chairman, Ronnie Lupe, a young university-educated man, spoke of the difficulties.

"Now on our reservation today, and much to our dismay in a way, modernism from the outside has complicated our everyday life. . . . In many instances confusion has set in and our behavior shows attitudes of defiance and depression."

On the reservation are many signs of the old and the new. Some of the Apaches live in wickiups (straw huts) or tents. Some live in privately built two- to five-room frame houses while others live in modern houses built with the aid of federal funds. Each fall, the White Mountain Apaches honor their heritage and their culture with an annual tribal fair and rodeo. During this fair, young girls are welcomed into the tribal society by special rites in a ceremony that stems from the early days of their culture. There is the old, with the ceremonial dances which have not changed through the centuries, and there is the new, in the modern western dances. The rodeo vies for public attention with the Indian exhibits of handicrafts:

White Mountain Apache Sunrise Dance, Arizona

beadwork, leatherwork, needlework in traditional patterns and designs, basketry and light woodwork.

The Apaches themselves feel that the lack of education of their people is the biggest problem they face. This is not just a question of receiving more funds from the federal government, which they are seeking, for expanded educational facilities. More important, they are trying to instill the tribal members with a belief in the *necessity* of education. Lupe has said that parents *must* encourage their youngsters to stay in school:

> We must explain to them the importance of becoming educated so that they can become accomplished leaders. . . . We can do a lot to help them become accomplished in both English and Apache. By knowing both ways they can in return help our tribe. . . .

The tribal leaders are trying to use the land to improve their economy. They have developed the largest privately owned recreation area in the western United States. It consists of more than 300 miles of trout streams and several lakes, including a man-made lake. The tribal-owned sawmill is large, and the Apaches are accomplished cattlemen. A deposit of low-grade iron is being explored in the northeast corner of the reservation.

And the tribe has been knowledgeable enough to seek out funds from the various federal agencies so that they can expand their activities. Too often tribes do not know how and where to go for federal funds which are available to them for development. Not so with the White Mountain Apaches, who have sought and received funds from such organizations as the Office of Economic Opportunity (OEO), the Economic Development Administration (EDA), Health, Education and Welfare (HEW), Bureau of Indian Affairs (BIA), Housing and Urban

Development (HUD). As a result of projects worked out with these funds, the overall unemployment rate is a very low 7 percent of the labor force over the year. But yet the monies coming in to each family during the year are far below the national poverty level: the average family income is only $500 to $1,000, with the majority closer to $500.

When he was seeking reelection as tribal chairman, Ronnie Lupe listed some of the things that had been done for self-betterment by the tribe under his direction: new homes, better roads, new community centers, better water and sanitation facilities, new schools, improved airport, a Head Start program for preschoolers, a bank on the reservation, assistance and support for the college potential (over 100 Apache youths are now enrolled in colleges and universities). A resort lodge and ski-lift complex are in the initial stages of construction.

It is certain that no matter what economic paths the White Mountain Apaches choose, they are determined to keep their integrity and culture. A tribal member spoke of this feeling when he noted that his Apaches view the future, poor or not, with "optimism as compared to the urbanized, technological, and industrialized man." The hope for the future was expressed as "the hope that we Apaches are not terminated and destroyed by a desperate dominating society." The White Mountain Apaches place their hope in their youth, for the youth have returned to the reservation with "pride and reinforced tribal thinking."

One of the most picturesque reservations in Arizona is that of the Havasupai tribe. This tribe lives in a small valley in a side canyon of the Grand Canyon, which can only be reached by an eight-mile hike, or horseback trip, down over rough canyon trails to the valley floor. The valley, which is hemmed in by rock walls 3,000 feet high, is level enough for farming, and there is water from creeks for crop irrigation. The beautiful Havasu River runs through the land, with three spectacular waterfalls, and many deep swimming pools. Two hundred and sixty-seven Indians live here, farming the land, growing corn, beans, squash and melons. They collect the harvest from peach, apricot, fig, apple, pear and pecan trees. The farming is still done in a rather primitive manner although the Havasupais have a tractor for plowing and leveling. Some plots are used for raising alfalfa and hay. The Indians own about 100 head of cattle and about 750 horses and mules. They rely on the tourist business for their largest source of income.

There is only one school on the reservation, for preschool, first- and second-grade children. Older students are sent to federal boarding schools. In this one school, there is one teacher, a caretaker and a cook. There is one church.

Although today the reservation is a Shangri-la, still relatively untouched by the white man's culture, there are signs that the old ways are changing. Recently three helicopters took off from the rim of the Grand Canyon and made the descent to the floor of the canyon. They carried in materials for five prefabricated homes. The houses included indoor plumbing and were wired for electricity. The families to receive these homes had been living in cardboard and tin houses. They had been chosen by the drawing of five names from a hat containing the names of thirteen of the tribe's most needy families. With great satisfaction, tribal chairman, Daniel Kaska, spoke of the new houses: "It's good that progress and development have finally come to my 267 people."

Other Arizona Indians who have found the old ways unsatisfactory for their well-being are those who live on the Gila River

Pima woman

Reservation, south of Phoenix. Here 7,000 Indians, mostly Pimas and a small group of Maricopas, farmed for many years; farming was their main source of livelihood. Then the water supply diminished, and the tribal leaders were forced to plan for the development of industry. They did such a superb job in their planning that today poverty and low incomes are not serious problems, but rather housing (most live in sandwich houses made of mud and board) and education are.

The tribe did not merely concentrate on bringing industry to the reservation, but started a new major bootstrap program of total development. This program, called *Vh-Thaw-Hup-Ea-Ju,* which means "It Must Happen," was launched five years ago, and included fifty-two projects of economic, social, community and government management development. The results of the program were truly significant. Three industrial parks were built, funded by the federal EDA. Most spectacular is their impressive building for tourists, which was opened in the summer of 1971, and which contains an arts and crafts shop and restaurant.

There are many problems, of course, still facing these Indians, but through their own efforts they have decided the direction the tribe must take. They retain some of the old culture, but they are eager to work and plan for a modern way, which they say is a better way of life for their people.

Another tribe in Arizona is that of the Colorado River Indians. They live on a small reservation nestled near the Colorado River and the border of California. The tribe of 1,800 Indians is almost exuberant in its well-being. Unemployment is virtually nonexistent, and incomes range as high as $40,000, with the average annual income varying between $3,000 and $6,500. There are 500 children in public elementary and high schools.

Constructing a main irrigation canal on the Colorado River Reservation in Arizona

credit: BIA

The health of the tribe is very good. There is a small hospital, with four trained doctors. Crafts are produced and marketed easily. Farming is especially successful, aided by extensive irrigation projects. There is a factory on the reservation which manufactures lawn furniture. And although more needs to be done in the field of housing, the tribe continues to progress in that area, with most of the Indians living in modern frame houses.

The tribe is most optimistic about the future, for they seem to be adapting their old ways to the best of the new. A spokesman said that the culture of the tribe has been retained in most cases, and at the same time the tribe is operating on a $1 million yearly budget. Presently, new land is being developed for agriculture, and since Parker Valley has such an excellent climate for farming, significant expansion can be expected. Tribal chairman, Dempsey Scott, is enthusiastic about the coming projects, and is quick to share credit with others for the progress that has been made. The people of the community, those who live on the river, and the Parker Chamber of Commerce have all worked with the Indians—and that factor, Scott feels, is why there has been such rapid development of the reservation.

5

THE INDIANS
OF NEW MEXICO

Among the Indians of New Mexico the situation of the Zuñis illustrates the difficulties encountered when people of an old culture are faced with the assimilation of the new.

Today the Zuñi Indian Pueblo, on the border of Arizona, has a population of almost 5,000 who live on about 407,000 acres of land.

World War II had a great impact on the Zuñis, for prior to it the Indians had little contact with the outside world. There were very few automobiles in the village, few roads and little communication with the outside. The Zuñis were self-contained, with a unique religion and culture, and an economy that was based primarily on the raising of sheep, the cultivation of small irrigated farms and on silversmithing. Very little money was used since most of the Zuñis traded for the goods they required.

Then came the war. Many Zuñis served in the armed forces where they were exposed to a life quite different from that of the reservation. After the war, the young Zuñis wanted more of the goods and services they had seen while serving their country. The resources on the reservation did not seem to be adequate. Newly paved roads made it possible for many Zuñis to find jobs off the reservation, and some left to relocate. So change brought more change.

Before World War II, the tribal council had always consisted of the older, more conservative and traditional men. But in the late 1950's younger, better-educated and more progressive leaders were elected, men who brought such innovations as water and sewage systems to the village.

However, by 1961, the impetus for change brought reaction: the Zuñis returned the older, traditional group to the council. That same year they voted at a general council meeting to reject industry on the reservation, showing reluctance to join the economic mainstream. Slowly though, minds changed again. Four years later the Indians voted to solicit industry which could provide jobs and opportunity to the Zuñi people, and, as a result, two small industries were brought to the reservation in 1967; providing over 100 jobs. The Bureau of Indian Affairs made available on-the-job training funds, which in turn made the Indian reservation even more attractive to industry.

Late in the 1960's, the Zuñis, now far from shunning outside contact, sought new sources of financial assistance. The days of reaction were over. The Zuñi tribe was one of the first Indian groups to apply successfully to the Office of Economic Opportunity for help, and with this came the tribe's first experience in managing a program which involved large amounts of money. They also received funds for a Community Action Program, Head Start, and received a $400,000 grant to establish an Arts and Crafts Cooperative and to train silversmiths.

Perhaps the biggest "industry" since the beginning of the twentieth century for the Zuñis has been, and is, silversmithing. The demand for the crafting of silver and turquoise is great, and this cottage industry exists today in almost every Zuñi home, at least as a supplemental source of income. With some Indians it is a full-time occupation. Silversmithing provides an income to the tribe estimated to be around $1,000,000.

More along the usual lines of American industry, the Zuñis have completed an industrial park, a community training center, and are building an airstrip, which should help the industrial, commercial, recreational and tourism development of the reservation. All these projects were supported both by Economic Development Assistance and the Zuñi Pueblo.

While the course of the Zuñis has been slow, part of the responsibility has been their own. Back in 1963, a Zuñi Housing Authority was established and the following year the Housing and Urban Development of the federal government approved thirty-five houses called "mutual help" homes (meaning that Indians did part of the work). Several years went by but construction did not begin. The Zuñis, although funds were available, did not decide until early 1967—three years later—that they wanted the houses. For in spite of all the advancement into the white man's culture, some Zuñis resisted. They saw the white culture and the culture of the Zuñis as conflicting. For example, under the Zuñi culture all of the daughters stay in the homes of their parents, even when married, resulting in extended family units. But the Housing and Urban Development program called for single dwelling units. The program was— and still is—in direct conflict with the traditional way of living. It took three years to persuade the Zuñis to accept this program for better housing. In 1967 construction was started on twelve housing units, and the thirty-five houses were completed in June, 1969. The program was accepted by the young. More homes were, and will be constructed, until there is a total of 850 new houses. Hopefully this will be accomplished by 1975.

What a vast change this represents, and on both sides. It was only in 1965 that a lawsuit by the Pine Ridge Indians of South Dakota forced the Housing Assistance Administration of the HUD to make housing funds available to all Indians. One could say, then, that the Zuñi "mutual help" housing represented a successful experiment for all concerned.

Yet with all this activity not so very many of the benefits of the new programs have filtered down to the individual Zuñi family. Average income is still far below that of the national American average. Some family heads who have full-time employment may have incomes ranging from $6,000 to $18,000 per year, but that is very exceptional. Zuñi health is poor, probably fifteen to twenty years behind the national health status. Medical services are available through government health service, but here again the differences in cultures create problems. Many Indians do not avail themselves of the health service, for they still believe in the medicine men and their own religious and cultural practices.

As far as education is concerned, over 2,000 Zuñi children attend public and parochial schools. On the higher level many Zuñi Indians have received grants to attend college. In spite of the fact that educational opportunities are available to the Zuñis, students are about three years behind those of comparable age in the white society. Again, it is not lack of facilities, but a difference in culture, and a lack of education experience on the part of the parents, who have only a limited view of the need and desirability of education.

Thus the Zuñis are really still part of two worlds: the "progress" of the present and the tradition and culture of the past. Perhaps because their culture is still important in their daily lives, they are a very stable tribe. As one BIA official said of the Zuñis:

> I hope our national goals will give them time to sort out of both cultures those things that are good and compatible with their developments and identity. I personally feel that Indians generally have come a long way in one hundred years. In many cases I feel they have been pushed too far too fast. We, the non-Indians, are the ones who need patience.

So it is patience and hope that will mold the future, and not only with the Zuñis. Although the conditions of the Indians vary greatly, almost all tribes express a similar hope for the future. Sometimes the hope seems justified by existing conditions or future potential; other times to a non-Indian, the hope seems almost wishful. Yet it is probably this very hope which will enable most Indian tribes to pull themselves into the world they want in the coming years.

Take the case of the Indians of the Cochiti Pueblo, where 450 (out of a tribal enrollment of 750) members live on the reservation, west of Santa Fe, New Mexico. Here, housing is primitive; the majority of the homes are adobe huts built by the Indians. Yet in the shadow of the adobes, there is planning and hope; a new program is under way and so far twenty-five homes have been built of concrete block, partially by the Indians, under a mutual self-help plan with the government (like the Zuñis). There are public schools on and off the reservation and a Bureau of Indian Affairs school.

While there is some farming on the reservation, there is no industry—yet. There are hopes for attracting industry, but most of the people are employed off the reservation. Three hundred Indians of working age are unemployed. The market is good for Cochiti crafts, but often the Indians have to sell their products at low prices to traders.

These Indians have their problems, but they are undaunted. One tribal spokesman said: "The future looks great for our community as far as progress is concerned. Our youth is being utilized to a great extent in getting involved in community functions."

Is the hope justified? Statistically the sociologists may wonder. But the Cochiti do not; they have hope.

North of the Cochiti lives a large grouping of Northern Pueblo Indians—among them the Taos, San Juan, Picuris, Santa Clara, Pojoaque, San Ildefonso, and Tesuque. As with so many, these Indians on the reservations are by no means prosperous: the average yearly income per family is still under $3,000; housing conditions are poor, but improving; job openings are not as numerous as they need to be; and alcoholism is a severe problem.

Yet, according to one Bureau of Indian Affairs official, in this area the Indian "is making great strides in solving his own problems in his own way. The Indian population is growing, becoming better educated, becoming more outspoken and no longer sits back for the Great White Father to make his decisions. All of these are healthy, positive, active signs in a culture that some people have felt was not moving." Hope again.

Of all the tribes in New Mexico, an outstanding example of one which has adapted to a modern society most successfully is that of the Jicarilla Apache (so called because of a unique

Taos Pueblo, New Mexico

credit: U.S. Forest Service

basket drinking cup they use). Theirs is a success story, but success has brought its own price tag; with the Jicarilla the adoption of technology and changed economy have been achieved at the expense of the culture of the tribe.

Five hundred years ago, the Jicarilla Apaches were warriors and buffalo hunters in the high mountain ranges and elevated lands along the Continental Divide in northern New Mexico. When the Spanish missionaries and conquerors came, there was much strife. The Jicarilla Apaches were pushed by the European settlers and other Indians from the area which is now eastern Colorado and western Kansas into land closer to the Pueblos. Here discord continued, although the Apaches began to adopt the Pueblo farming and living ways. In 1887, the Jicarilla Reservation was established, and the Indians settled down to using the land for grazing and forest, and for a range–livestock industry.

Today these Indians lead a far different life from their lives five centuries ago. Sheep and cattle still graze, the forest still provides timber, but the Indians have found and have helped exploit far greater natural resources on the 742,000 acres of the reservation. The land is dotted with natural gas wells and oil wells, and contains one of the state's largest untapped supplies of underground water.

"If I sound conceited," the tribal secretary remarked recently, "it is because I am very proud of my tribe and the accomplishments they have made over the past twenty years. Before the 1950's we were a very poor lot of people, but because of the oil and gas development on the reservation and the sound investments of these monies, we are where we are."

The Jicarilla Apaches—there are 1,750 members—have accepted the white man's technology and agricultural innova-

Christmas Dance, Tesuque Pueblo, New Mexico

tions. In the beginning of the 1970's, the tribe was worth over $10 million.

The tribe owns an electronics plant. Its Dulce Lake Recreation area, a tribal enterprise, is an extremely successful attraction for tourists. The tribe has a $1 million scholarship fund for those tribal members who wish to go to college. The youngsters —and about 1,000 of the tribal members are under twenty-five years of age—have good opportunities for education.

The tribe invested in a motion picture, which was filmed largely in New Mexico, starring Kirk Douglas and Johnny Cash. In addition, the Jicarilla Apaches recently received grants from the government for the establishment of Elk Game Park, the building of a motel and more recreational facilities. These are aggressive Indians, in tune with the times, and the efforts of the tribe, guided by its council, have brought a higher standard of living to its members than almost any other Indian tribe.

The average annual income is $4,600, well above that of the majority of Indian tribes. Most of the Indians live within fifteen miles of the town of Dulce, in log cabins, pumice block and frame houses, most of which were privately financed. There has been a good deal of home construction in the last few years, aided by government funds. The adults work at all kinds of jobs from laborers to administrative managers. Many are employed by the tribe, the Bureau of Indian Affairs or the Public Health Service. They also make beadwork and basketry, which are sold to the tribe and resold to the tourists.

A public school was built on the reservation in 1957, at which time the Indian boarding school was closed. About forty Jicarilla Apache students attend other schools in New Mexico, Utah, Arizona, Colorado, and Oklahoma, because their parents

Basket weaving from yucca leaves

feel that the local school system is not academically challenging enough.

The Jicarilla Apache tribe has adopted modern methods of industry and is prospering. But here is the price: the Jicarilla Apaches are slowly losing the customs of their tribe. There is little left of their past. Only a few traditional ceremonies remain, nothing more.

Like many Indian tribes, the Jicarilla Apaches do not have a hospital on the reservation, but are served by a small outpatient clinic, staffed by two doctors and a dentist. But unlike many tribes, the Jicarillas have submitted a proposal for a Public Health Service Indian Community Hospital, with a capacity of thirty-two beds, at a cost of almost $2 million to construct and equip, to serve the Indian and non-Indian population within a fifty-mile radius of Dulce. There is a good chance that this hospital will be a reality in the near future.

The majority of the Jicarilla Apache tribe feels that its biggest problems are to secure further industrial development, hospital facilities, a jail, a better sewer system and employment. All these are very modern needs. In meeting them one factor is tied to another, and most are based on available funds. They believe that the future holds only "the best" for them. But one spokesman noted that they are "caught within two worlds" and some Indians "find the adjustment difficult." They "give up in despair, cannot revert back to former days and Indian ways." But the majority feels that the tribe is being placed "in the position of having a place in the sun."

6

THE INDIANS OF CALIFORNIA

Unlike the reservations in Arizona, most of those in California are small, and some are even unoccupied.

The Indians are, however, ancient residents of California. They came to that area thousands of years ago; it has been estimated that at the time the first Spaniards pushed into California, there were between 133,000 and 150,000 Indians. Today, only about 40,000 Indians live in California, and of that number perhaps only 7,000 could be classified as "California Indians," the rest having come from New Mexico, Arizona and the Dakotas.

In the beginning the native Indians lived simply, needing only clothing and shelter in the warm climate. Those, in the south, ground acorns into meal and made their homes and utensils of intricate basketwork. Those, in the north, made their homes out of slabs from the redwood forests and were hunters and fishermen. There were some tribes who lived on the coast of California, but these coastal maritime Indians now appear to be extinct.

The coming of the white man created a special type of Indian —the Mission Indian, of whom there are several bands today. The Spanish built the missions, imposed the laws and generally took care of the Indians who came to live around them. Some tribes took as the tribal name that of the mission where they lived. About 20,000 to 25,000 Indians adopted this way of life. Other Indians in the south who were not attracted to the farming of the padres ignored the missions, and were known as the "wild" Indians. The mission system flourished for some years, but in the early part of the nineteenth century, the Indian population slowly declined, and the missions collapsed.

Then, the Indians in California were troubled by other new settlers. At the end of the war with Mexico, in 1848, California was ceded to the United States, and the gold rush began. The white men came, eager for gold, and with absolutely no regard for the Indians or their lands. They made treaties with the Indians, which they did not respect and through legal and illegal means, the Indians lost more and more land. By the time the General Allotment Act of 1887, which opened much of the land which had been Indian to the white homesteaders, was passed, the Indians in California were generally landless. Public attention was called to the miserable conditions of the Indians, and the Mission Relief Act of 1891 was passed, setting aside parcels of generally poor land for those Indians who had remained together as bands.

In the years following the Mission Relief Act, more laws were passed which provided money to buy small tracts of land in central and northern-central California for the Indians without land. Today these small tracts still form the bulk of the Indian lands—they are called "rancherias." These rancherias have suffered through the years from the termination impetus, and over thirty-five of them have lost the special relationship with the federal government, and more are presently preparing for termination.

Currently there are about 100 reservations and rancherias in California. Altogether these lands total over half a million acres and vary in size from less than one acre to the 87,000 acres of the Hoopa Valley Reservation. Yet many Indians do not live on this land. A number of the reservations were formed from lands so completely unsuitable to farming that hundreds of Indians drifted away from the reservations. Some went to the cities, particularly Los Angeles and San Diego, and today they live in residential areas like any other citizens.

On the rancherias and on the reservations the status of the land varies greatly. Some of it is held in trust by the federal government, other parts are individual allotments and some land is in the public domain. Many of the reservations are quite small, badly organized, and have boundary problems.

Those Indians who live on trust lands are still eligible for federal aid and the assistance of the Bureau of Indian Affairs. The government has brought water to many of the reservations for irrigation, and the Indians who remain on these lands have good gardens, and almond, apricot and cherry orchards. Other land provides good range for cattle and sheep. In the south, in addition to tending sheep, the Indians harvest crops on the large ranches owned by whites, as well as grow their own crops.

The Indians who stayed on the reservations are not well off. According to one Bureau official, the majority of these Indians are extremely poor and dependent upon welfare services for their existence. In one area in 1971, there were 9,084 acres of Indian land suitable for farming. Of this, 7,116 acres were not farmed and 544 acres were being used by non-Indians. BIA officials say the reasons for this nonuse are lack of irrigation facilities, multi-owned lands through heirship, allotments too small to be profitable and a "lack of interest" in farming on the part of the Indians. The BIA tries to help these Indians develop and manage their property so that they can be put "on equal footing with other citizens in the state."

The Indians are also helped in the area of housing. In the beginning of 1970, the first Indian Housing Authority in California was formed, and all Mission Indian reservations in southern California were invited to join. One of the first goals of this group was to build at least 100 homes.

Many of these Mission Indians today are distrustful of the Bureau, and fearful of the termination theory—in spite of government announcements that this policy has been ended. Often, too, these Indians are resentful of the Bureau, because it does not have sufficient federal appropriations to carry out all its announced programs. For example, for many years the social services that were given to Indians in other states were denied to the Indians of California. These services are now being restored, or planned for the future. California Indian students can again gain admission to Bureau boarding schools, and get scholarships and loans. Recently the federal government has been furnishing water and sewage facilities on many of the reservations. Planned for the future is the restoration of dental and medical care.

Today, the greatest needs of the Indians of California are for more funds to help them with their progress, and more cooperation among the various Indian groups. As one official said, the inability of these Indians to organize and therefore speak out in a much stronger voice is a current drawback. However, "there are indications now that there is more of a realization to do something about working together." In the last few years, more and more organizations of Indians in California have been established, and as a result, they are being heard.

Of course, not all of the California reservations have a great potential but many do, and they could provide employment for other Indians. In this respect, help can be given to the Indians by informing them of the various programs, sponsored by the federal, state and county governments for all citizens, not just Indians. The Indians must take advantage of these offers. As one non-Indian commented about the Indians with whom he was working, "they must learn to live for the future and not dwell on the injustices of the past."

Among the Indians in southern California is the Cabazon Band of Mission Indians. There are only twenty-four of them, all living on the reservation. One family lives in a mobile home, and the other in a three-bedroom home. All the children attend public school. All of working age are employed, One is self-employed, two are employed by the telephone company, one is a salesman and two are laborers. The average annual income for this group is $4,000, higher than the general Indian average. There are no industries on the reservation and no federal aid has been sought for any as yet. They do not farm anymore, nor follow the crafts of the old culture. This tribe, whose members are competing in a white society, feels, however, that it has retained its culture and identity as a tribe. It is true that the tribe has its own tribal bylaws, and since it still has a special relationship with the federal government, it adheres to federal laws. Here again is a tribe that claims great optimism for the future, in spite of the many problems it faces today. A tribal representative summed up the feeling of these Indians: "We hope that in the future, which looks very good, that the tribe as a whole will prosper very well."

A very different situation exists for the Chukchansi tribe, which no longer has any special relationship with the federal government, since termination in October, 1961. One can understand why, when one learns that at that time the tribe on the reservation consisted of only one family: a mother, a son and a daughter. With termination, the tribe became the owners of the land.

Recently the daughter wrote about her tribe from Coarsegold, California, showing a good deal about these Indians today:

> I would say there are around thirty [in the tribe], maybe a little more. Of course now they are mixed with other tribes. . . . I am the only one living now on the reservation. My mother was the only one that used to make baskets and bead work. I have still kept up the bead work I now sell; and sometimes I enjoy it. Basket? I don't know, I may pick it up later. I have six children; three girls and three boys. I have taught my girls how to make bead necklaces and brushes and other small things. I hate to see our culture die away. It seems like no one is interested in it.

As a P.S. she added: "I married a Mexican and there goes the tribe, but I am a Chukchansi. My mother and father were. . . ."

This Indian woman lives in a "regular house," and her children go to the local public school at Coarsegold where there are three teachers and about sixty-two students. The employed

Indians do lumber mill work, but the tribe no longer functions as a "tribe," for all its members take care of themselves, and the "tribe cannot get together as one." The biggest hope this Indian has is to see her grown children have "good schooling, and a good education." One might say then, that the Chukchansi tribe has refused to offer any "Indian" problem at all, that the tribe has been assimilated in general society, for better or worse.

Yet where tribes have remained an entity some have prospered. The Agua Caliente Band of Mission Indians are notable for their ownership of ten square miles of land within the celebrated desert resort city of Palm Springs. This group of Cahuilla Indians is small, with only about 150 members, but they have 32,000 acres, and are often spoken of as being "land rich." Their property, which they lease out most profitably, is extremely valuable.

As one of the Bureau officials said recently, as a result of their lease income, "the members of this band enjoy greater continuing financial benefits than almost any other Indians whose lands are held in trust by the federal government."

It was not always so. The reservation was created by a series of executive orders and by act of Congress in the late 1800's. This desert reservation was called "absolutely worthless" by an agent of the Bureau of Indian Affairs in 1912. Fifty years later the same land was appraised at more than $50 million by the Bureau.

The Indian land is exempt from taxation, and the city of Palm Springs is located within the boundaries of the reservation. Today many of the fine hotels and country clubs are on Indian lands which have been leased for from sixty-five to ninety-nine years.

There are still conflicts with the city of Palm Springs over zoning and the development of Indian versus non-Indian lands, but, according to one Bureau official, the future certainly looks good for the rich Agua Caliente Indians and "members of the band will influence and contribute to the development of Palm Springs for generations to come."

How could they do otherwise? As the largest single landowner in the Palm Springs area, with ten square miles within the city limits, with the remaining sections fanning out across the desert south and east, even mounting the sheer slopes of the San Jacinto Mountains on the west, this band cannot fail to prosper in this recreational oasis.

7

THE INDIANS
OF THE NORTHWEST

Over the years of settlement of the West, the Indians of the northwest, in the tri-state area of Oregon, Washington, and Idaho, fought hard against the invasion of the white man and consequently lost considerable amounts of their original territory. This area, split by the Cascade Mountain range running the length of Washington and Oregon, was inhabited to the east by the "plateau" Indians, the Nez Percé, Shoshones, Bannocks, Coeur d'Alenes, Kalispels, Yakimas, Spokanes, Klamaths and Colvilles. They were hunting people and many of them became horse dealers and breeders as "civilization" touched them. By the time the Oregon territory was officially established (1849) these Indians were often called the "horse Indians" as distinct from those on the other, coastal side of the mountain range, who were called the "canoe Indians."

The coastal Indians, among them the Quinaults, Quileutes, Makahs, Chinooks and Clallams, were fishermen and skilled craftsmen who used wood from the abundant forests.

With the coming of the white man, the Indians became fur traders and trappers. But as elsewhere, white settlement brought Indian decline and resentment. Treaties not honored, wars, and the gold rush to the northwest in the middle of the nineteenth century only made conditions more critical. Then many of the established reservations were thrown open to white settlers, and the Indians fought with the settlers, but in 1880 almost all of the surviving Indians of both groups in the tri-state area had gone to reservations without further resistance. So their modern history began.

Today in Oregon there are two Indian tribes that are excellent examples of the devastation caused by termination, on the one hand, and the progress permitted when a tribe is able to retain the special trustee relationship with the federal government on the other.

The Klamaths, in southern Oregon, were terminated in 1961. Today they are selling off by auction the last of the tribe's land to the highest bidder.

An anguished Klamath Indian leader who opposed the sale of the remaining 145,000 acres of pine forest, mountain pasture, and ranchland of the tribe spoke out: "We're robbing our own children," he said, ". . . what kind of people are we?"

Over a century ago the Klamaths (then numbering 1,200) held territory larger than West Virginia. They signed a treaty with President Ulysses S. Grant, giving all but a million acres of that land to the federal government; in return, they received a reservation from which whites were barred, an annual payment to the tribal treasury, and promises of training in the white man's agriculture and education. The Klamaths settled down to live peacefully on the reservation. In time they began receiving some monies from the federal government for timber

logged on the reservation. By the middle of the twentieth century, in the termination era, Congress decided that the Klamath
tribe could and should handle its own affairs. It ordered the
Department of the Interior to begin preparing for termination
of the reservation. During this time, almost 80 percent of the
tribal members voted to convert their interests into cash.

The remaining members elected to hold their interests in
common under a management trust, but by 1969 these
Klamaths voted to dissolve the trust. They complained that the
management fee was too high for the individual Indians, who
received only about $1,500 in annual income. So the land was
set to be sold.

If the present governmental policy against termination had
only been in effect a few years ago, perhaps the Klamath Indians would still be an active healthy tribe. It has become all too
clear that the majority of Indians want to keep, and need, a
special relationship with the federal government, so they may
have federal assistance as they try to rebuild their tribes. In
recent years the Indians have indicated that they want to develop their land, improve their economy, and as individual
groups provide for the betterment of their people. They, and all
the rest of us, have seen the results of the "new colonialism"
represented by the termination policy. It is hard to visualize the
termination of the Klamaths in today's climate of recognition
of Indian rights and hopes.

In contrast to the Klamaths, now landless, are the Indians
on the Warm Springs Reservation in the northwestern part of
Oregon, who have not been terminated. Here about 1,400 Indians of various tribes—the Taih, Wyam, Tenino and Dochapus
of the Walla Wallas, the Ki-gal-twal-la, the Dalles and the Dog
River of the Wascoes, and a small band of Paiutes—live on or

near the reservation. Most of the land is tribally owned and held in trust by the federal government. With this land as an economic base, the tribes (under their own community government) have done an amazing job in developing their reservation.

The tribes own and operate the *Kah-Nee-Ta* (Gift of the Gods) resort, a $5 million mineral springs resort on the reservation. This complex of lodges, campsites, spring-fed swimming pools, and fishing areas has great attraction for the West Coast tourist, and has become a great money-maker—so much so that a $4.3 million expansion of the facilities is currently under way.

The tribe also owns and operates their own sawmill, veneer mill, and plywood lay-up plant. They own and operate an electronic subassembly plant which employs many of the Indians. The tribes have placed over a million dollars in a revolving credit fund for housing and another half-million dollars is being set aside for the home ownership program.

All these projects have been accomplished by the Indians themselves. The results of proper land management by the Indians are most satisfying on this reservation. A recent survey showed that only a little over 3 percent of the tribal members had an income of less than $1,000. Over 8 percent had incomes of $10,000 and over. The highest percentage (over 13 percent) were in the income categories of $4,000–$5,000 and $5,000–$6,000. ("Income" for these Indians includes a monthly per person payment by the tribes to all of the members.)

These Indians, with what one BIA official calls "outstanding leadership," have been willing and capable of working with all types of government and private resources to accomplish their own tribal aims. The results are obvious in the relatively high incomes received by the Indians.

Kah-Nee-Ta resort on the Warm Springs Reservation, Oregon

credit: BIA

In the State of Washington there are special Indian problems that are due to geography and, in part, to what the white man calls "progress."

The twenty-two Indian reservations in Washington vary in size from those of a few hundred acres like Shoalwater, to three comparatively large reservations, the Colville, Yakima, and Spokane. These tribes have a number of similar problems, such as: isolation (many are miles away from developed towns and communities); too little land; improper use of land; and difficulties over fishing rights.

Some of the Indians on the Washington reservations have adopted the white man's ways and have been assimilated into white society. Such is the case of those Indians on the smallest of the coastal reservations, the Shoalwater. This reservation consists of only 334 acres and was established in 1866, not for a specific tribe (because there are no "Shoalwater Indians"), but in the catchall "for miscellaneous Indian purposes."

In the past many members of the various tribes lived on the reservation, but today there are only eight families, with a total of twenty-two members . These people, although they are at this writing in the process of drawing up a tribal constitution and bylaws, live as do their white neighbors. The adults work in the surrounding non-Indian community, in the cranberry bogs, and in fishing and crabbing. The Indians here all speak good English, all read and write, and their children attend nearby public schools. Thus, these Indians are truly a part of the white community. One could scarcely say they have "Indian problems" except cultural ones.

The Indians north of the Shoalwater, on the Quinault Reservation, are also fairly well integrated into the non-Indian community. By and large they too have adopted the white man's ways, in spite of retaining a few of their own traditions such as Indian dances, salmon barbecues, and canoe races. For over three generations, tribal children have attended white schools and all but a few of the older Indians speak and understand English.

The reservation here is the largest in western Washington, containing almost 190,000 acres, but most of the land is not owned by the tribe as a whole. It is either owned by logging companies, or has been allotted to individual Indians and held in trust for them. The western boundary of this beautiful reservation is the Pacific Ocean, and the land rises eastward to the foothills of the Olympic Mountains. There are many clear streams and high clay and sandstone bluffs, and Lake Quinault, six miles square, is wholly within the reservation.

About 1,000 Quinaults live here, mainly in the villages of Taholah and Queets. Usually they live in frame houses of from two to six rooms, and the conditions of the houses vary widely as far as upkeep and modernization are concerned. They receive their incomes from timber sales, land rentals, fishing, or employment in logging, canneries and agriculture. The timberland which is the major resource on the reservation is sufficient to provide individuals with personal incomes from their land for some years to come, but unfortunately on the land that is owned as a whole by the tribe, the timber will be mostly cut in the next few years. Some other way will have to be devised to bring in money for tribal programs. Studies show that a fish hatchery on the reservation would be feasible, and there is a possibility of tourist–recreational development, but this can be undertaken only when enough highways are built through the reservation. This may be a long time in coming.

Nearby, the Hoh Reservation suffers problems caused by

isolation. It is small (443 acres), on the coast of the Pacific, and the nearest town, twenty-five miles to the north, is Forks where their children attend school and where medical and dental care are available. The reservation houses only about fifteen to thirty permanent residents who live in a fishing village at the mouth of the Hoh River. Fishing for a living is becoming more difficult each year, since the fish runs are steadily declining. Several of the Indians still make the traditional Indian canoes for river and ocean use, and several of the women make baskets, so a little money comes in from the sale of crafts to tourists.

Only recently—1969—a constitution was adopted for the tribes and a tribal council elected. It was "too late" as far as regulation of the exploitation of the reservation was concerned: the reservation had been logged off in 1954 in the old careless way, and now it will be forty to sixty years before a second timber growth will be of much commercial value. The reservation does have a mile of ocean beach front, but this would have to be developed into a tourist attraction to be of much economic use. Thus the Indians on the Hoh Reservation now live a fairly self-contained existence, but they have a difficult time ahead, for the fishing cannot support them in the future as well as it has in the past.

Another tribe that suffers from the serious problem of isolation is that of the Makah whose reservation is far north, bordered by the Pacific Ocean on the west, and by the Straits of Juan de Fuca on the north. These straits separate the reservation from Vancouver Island. The nearest towns are Forks, forty-nine miles southeast, and Port Angeles, seventy-two miles east. The reservation has miles of sandy beach, and heavily timbered mountains. Much of the area is untouched—a boon for the future, but a problem at the moment.

There is great potential for the land of the Makah tribe, for the 515 members own almost 90 percent of the 27,000 acres. The land is valuable for its timber, and luckily the Makah tribe has used good judgment about the cutting. It has been well planned so that there are good remaining timber resources, unlike those of the Quinaults. There are also deposits of manganese, asphalt and granite which could in the future be exploited commercially. The best mineral resource of all on their land is the deposits of paving gravel, however, it is impossible to develop at present because of the distance from markets and the poor condition of the roads on the reservation. When these roads are improved, and if U.S. Highway 101 is extended through the village of Neah Bay as proposed, these potential assets can be developed. Also, with improved roads, tourism and recreational facilities could be developed by the tribe, for just off the coast of the reservation is some of the finest salmon fishing water in the northwest.

Today most of the tribal members live in the village of Neah Bay, and in small settlements at Sekiu and Clallam Bay, twenty miles to the east. They earn their incomes from fishing, lumbering, and from rental of their individual land allotments. Little can be done in the field of agriculture, since the land is heavily wooded, so the Makah engage in personal subsistence gardening, and only a limited amount of grazing livestock. Some of the Indians own small commercial fishing vessels, which they were able to buy through tribal financing. Extra income comes from the sale of Indian arts and crafts—wood carvings, knitting, beadwork, basketry and canoes.

Living conditions on the reservation are fairly primitive; most of the cottage-type homes have inside plumbing and septic tanks, but waste disposal and drainage are problems for some.

A plan has been drawn up for an adequate water and sewage system for Neah Bay, but it will have to be constructed in stages. In general, housing also needs to be greatly improved.

Twenty years ago the Makah tribe made a claim with the Indian Claims Commission for $10 million, for the loss of fishing rights and land, but then the commission decided no payment was due to the tribe. Today, however, the tribe has renewed the claim and has employed an attorney to prosecute the case for them. Perhaps, with the change in American public opinion about the rights of Indians, the Makah may receive some compensation for lost land, as have many other Indian tribes.

The Makah are still concerned, however, with their fishing rights. They were the ones who started the phenomenon called the "Fish-Ins." Fish-Ins were fishing excursions off the reservations, without licenses—acts of civil disobedience against the game laws.

Early in 1964 the Makahs decided that the tribes in the state, which were small and scattered for the most part, could not win their fishing rights until they all got together. They did so, with the aid of the National Indian Youth Council who looked upon their participation in the Fish-In as their first direct action.

The problem of the fishing rights of the Washington Indian tribes is extremely critical, for fishing is the main source of livelihood for those Indians on or near the water. The dispute arises from a century-old breach of promise: in the Treaty of Medicine Creek signed by the United States and the Indians in 1854, the government severely reduced the land holdings of the Indians, but the treaty guaranteed the "right" of the Indians to fish in the rivers, in the "usual and accustomed grounds." Again in other treaties, with the tribes of the coastal regions of

Puget Sound, land was given up, but the fishing "rights" were retained.

Over the years, with the shrinking of the reservations, the "usual and accustomed" grounds were not always available, so the Indians began fishing off the reservation. In the nineteenth century this did not matter greatly, for with simple fishing equipment, poles and nets, the catch was small. However, the Indians learned from the whites and with the modern method of gill netting they began to increase their catch. Fishing became profitable. In recent years, it has been estimated that the Indians took 30 percent of the fish caught on the rivers in Washington. The Yakimas alone (who number around 7,000 and live on a reservation north of the Columbia River, bordered by the Yakima River) netted about 15 percent of the fish caught on the Upper Columbia.

As sport fishing and tourism grew in Washington, so did white commercial fishing corporations. At the same time, there was a decrease in salmon runs and the whites saw that on the coastal rivers and along Puget Sound some 75 percent of the Indians were earning much of their basic livelihood by fishing. (Twenty-five percent of the income of the Yakimas and the Columbia River tribes, it has been estimated, depended on their fish catches.)

So the State of Washington looked to its rules and regulations, in the interest of the "conservation" of the fish. In 1963, the Supreme Court of Washington State decided against the Indians: the court decreed that "none of the signatories of the original treaty [Treaty of Medicine Creek, with the Indians] contemplated fishing with 600-foot nylon gill net, which could prevent the escapement of any fish for spawning purposes."

This decision then led the Indians to take action on their

own: the Fish-Ins. Fishing off the reservations began. The results could have been predicted: the game wardens made arrests, on the Quillayute River, on the Puyallup River, the Yakima River, the Nisqually River, the Columbia River, and the Green River. Before the Fish-Ins ended, there were thousands of Indians—from fifty-six tribes throughout the country —participating. The Indians were determined to win back their old rights. The treaties had been made in perpetuity—for "as long as the grass grows and the rivers run," yet the officials of the state felt that they could not permit "uncontrolled or unregulated fishery by the Indians. . . ." But to the Indians, forever was forever, not just so long as might be convenient for the whites.

Clashes between the Indians and authority had been going on sporadically for years, but never before the 1960's had there been such organized protest. The results of the Fish-In were surprising—and gratifying—to the Indians: representatives of the Federal Department of Justice appeared before the Supreme Court of Washington State "in behalf of a tribe which had been enjoined from exercising its fishing rights." For nearly—if not actually—the first time, the government was defending the tribes' rights in a treaty made with the government.

The assistant attorney general of the United States wrote to the National Indian Youth Council that the Department of Justice was determined "to defend the treaty rights of the Indian tribes" and that they would defend on request any individual Indians who were fishing in accordance with the treaty and tribal regulations, if they were charged by the state with violation of the state's fish and game laws. Thus, the Department of Justice went on record as planning to insure that various tribes could "pursue their treaty fishing free from outside interference."

That was a beginning. But to the Indians it was not nearly enough. In addition to preserving their fishing rights, the Indians want the government to give technical assistance and fishery management services to the tribes. They want federal funds for tribal fish-conservation programs and for tribal development of commercial and sports fishing. Such help alone could put the tribes on a firm economic footing.

The Indians want a federal appropriation of $100,000 for these programs, and according to one Indian leader, that is not much considering everything, for twice that amount is being made available by the federal Bureau of Commercial Fisheries to *non-Indian* commercial fishing and industrial interests. And the Indian people of that area are impoverished, while the non-Indian interests are economically well-established.

At the time of the federal government's intervention with the State of Washington and their proclamation that they would defend the treaty rights of the Indians, the Vietnam war was in full swing. When asked for help by the Indians, the government officials invoked the priority needs of the war. Thus, it was with surprise that these Indians learned that a civic action program was under way in Vietnam, a program that was assisting the Vietnamese in a big fisheries development, one that dwarfed the needs of the American Indians. The Indians did not necessarily begrudge aid to the fishermen of Saigon, but why could they not get help at home? During the Fish-Ins, when the State of Washington was confiscating hundreds of fishing nets and scores of boats and motors, the United States was, according to the Indians, supplying nearly 10,000 outboard motors, 50,000 sets of fishing gear, 27,000,000 fingerlings for stocking purposes, and building sixteen fishing piers for the Vietnamese. It still remains to be seen how much help these Indians will receive for a fisheries program.

Not all of the tribes in Washington are dramatically concerned with the fishing rights of the Indians. Many of them have very special problems which are related to either the loss of land or the use of the remaining land. Case after case can be cited of those Indian tribes that had land, and now have practically none, so many that the recitation becomes numbing. For examples are the following: The Puyallup tribes had a reservation created under the Treaty of Medicine Creek, which was in the area of present-day Tacoma, where land is valued in thousands of dollars by the lot, not just the acre. The Puyallups have today three acres in all—a tribal cemetery, and a few scattered lots owned by the tribe all within the city of Tacoma.

The Muckleshoots, north of the Puyallups, have a reservation, but more than two of the over 3,000 acres are owned by non-Indians. The tribally owned lands consist of about one-quarter of an acre on which the community hall is located.

On Puget Sound is the Port Madison Reservation, which originally consisted of 7,284 acres; today it is only 2,680, and only forty-one of those are tribally owned. So the story is repeated time and time again; the Indians in Washington once had a great deal of land, yet today many are land poor.

The problems caused by the lack of land owned by the tribe as a whole can be illustrated by the case of the Skokomish Indian Reservation, which borders on Hoods Canal, with the south and southeast boundaries formed by the Skokomish River. When the reservation was established in 1855, there were about 5,000 acres. Of these, today only nineteen acres are owned in common by the tribe, and they consist of a school site and two cemetery sites. A total of a little over 3,000 acres is owned by individual Indians, and held in trust for them. But because the tribe itself has no land upon which to build as a tribe, it has practically no income, and thus cannot help itself.

Conditions on the reservation are relatively poor. Housing is substandard—most of the houses are overcrowded and provide only the most minimal protection when there is heavy rainfall or occasional heavy snowfall. The poor heating and ventilation contributes to respiratory infections and other illness. A number of families still carry or haul their water for domestic use from contaminated or potentially contaminated sources. Collection and disposal of garbage are irregular. The open dumps breed rats, insects, and disease. The Division of Indian Health of the federal government is currently trying to institute programs to raise the low health level but there is far to go to erase poverty and misery here.

These Indians are "helped" by the federal government, but luckily they are under state legal jurisdiction except for treaty hunting and fishing. (They have, of course, their own constitution and bylaws, and a tribal council which decides on tribal matters.) It is fortunate that they are under state jurisdiction, because then they, like many of the other Washington tribes, receive state and community services, such as library bookmobile, child welfare, and other economic relief and public education. Although by and large the tribe is classed as literate, the educational level of the tribe as a whole is lower than that of some of the tribes in the surrounding area, and although more Skokomish students now attend secondary schools than before, the dropout rate is very high.

One of the difficulties for those Indians who own their land is that its condition often makes farming difficult. Some 1,000 acres is rich river bottomland, but this is subject to flooding, and there are serious drainage problems. Dikes are needed, as are draining ditches and pumping stations.

Hay is the major cash crop and dairying is the major source of income. Other crops include grain, berries and fruit. Fishing is very important for during the winter months fish, clams, and oysters provide the 150 residents with part of their food supply, along with deer and wild fowl. A few of the Skokomish also try to add to their incomes by trapping beaver, muskrats, and mink.

Some of the Indians of Washington have become vocal and insistent about having the land that was taken from them returned now. The most interesting recent illustration involves the Nisqually Reservation, which is today only a fraction of what it once was. It is situated on the west side of the Nisqually River, with Olympia ten miles to the west, and Tacoma twenty miles to the northeast. This reservation, like many in Washington, was created as a result of the Medicine Creek Treaty of 1854, and by executive order in 1857. Originally it consisted of 4,717 acres, but the U.S. government, through the War Department, took over about 3,353 acres on the east side of the river, for Fort Lewis. After that, other land fell into non-Indian hands, and today there are only 833 acres of allotted land in trust or restricted for the Indians. The tribe as a whole now owns only two and a half acres, which is used as a cemetery.

It is not surprising the Indians bear resentment about the treatment they received from the whites, and no wonder they are seeking the return of their lands. In the spring of 1970, at Fort Lewis, actress Jane Fonda and thirteen other persons were arrested by the military police, after an attempt by about 150 Indians to occupy land at Fort Lawton, which was called a "satellite base of Fort Lewis."

The public attempt to seize land that once belonged to the Indians was sponsored by a recently formed Indian group: United American Indian Fort Lawton Occupational Force. This group climbed over fences, scaled a high bluff and set up a tepee on the fort grounds. The Indians demanded that an Indian university and cultural center be developed at the fort. The issue had erupted when part of the land was scheduled to be made army surplus, which meant that these lands which once belonged to the Indians could fall into non-Indian hands.

Nothing concrete was gained by this episode, but it did point up the smoldering resentment of the Indians against the grabbing of their lands through the years. Today, on the remaining land of the Nisqually Reservation there are twenty-three Nisquallys, with 166 Indians living nearby. They make their living mainly from fishing on the Nisqually River and from seasonal employment. Their condition today is a sad commentary on the past land acquisition programs of the federal government.

To speak positively for a change, it is good to report that the Spokanes in Washington are, as a tribe, on their feet economically because they did protest about land they had lost and the price the government had paid for that land back in the nineteenth century.

The original lands occupied by the Spokanes consisted of some 3 million acres along the Spokane River and the surrounding area. In 1880 about 3,000 Spokane Indians lived there. The years took their toll in land and people: wars, white homesteading, sale to government and power companies—all this "progress" depleted the Indian land area. Today the Spokane Reservation consists of 138,000 acres, 97,000 of them owned by the tribe, the rest by individual Indians.

After the Indian Claims Commission was created in 1946, to settle all claims filed by various tribes against the federal government, many of the tribes throughout the country, including the Spokanes, availed themselves of this service. In 1951, the Spokanes filed a claim alleging that the amount of money paid for the cession of land under an old agreement of 1887 was unreasonably low, and after years of legal battles, the lawyer for the Spokanes suggested a settlement, which was accepted by the tribal members at the end of 1966. Early the next year this settlement of $6.7 million was approved by the Claims Commission, and a few months later President Lyndon B. Johnson signed the bill appropriating these funds, on condition that the tribe draw up a reasonable plan for the use of the money. The plan was made, and the government agreed: one-half of the settlement, roughly $3 million, would go to individual tribal members ($1,750 to each adult member), and the rest would be used for reservation development.

This compensation for the old land sales has made a tremendous difference in the economic situation of the Spokane. There is enough money to work with so the tribal council recently appointed a fifteen-man task force to recommend a program for development of reservation resources. Uranium deposits were found and mined, providing new income and new jobs. The tribe hopes that many more profitable mines can be found and exploited. To this end a Denver mining concern has leased thousands of acres of reservation land and is carrying on an extensive exploration program.

As far as the individual Indians on the reservation are concerned, about one-third of the tribe, or 700 people, are fairly well off. Most have seasonal jobs in logging and mining, and although these industries are owned by outside interests, the jobs and rents provide income to the tribe. The percentage of unemployed is very small and the estimated average income is about $4,000, quite high compared to the national Indian average. Some of the Spokanes farm to supplement their incomes, but these are small operations, although they include some successful cattle ranching. Most of those who do not live on the reservation live and work in the nearby city of Spokane.

The Spokane tribe has retained a little of the old culture through ceremonial dances and traditional games, but the native language is slowly being lost. As usual, the old crafts are still practiced by some of the tribe, and the products are marketed individually by the members.

In retaining even a small part of the old culture, the Spokanes show a far different picture from the Coeur d'Alene tribe in Idaho. These Indians, too, have embraced industrialization, but nearly all the old culture of the tribe has been abandoned and today none of the old crafts are produced by the tribe. Here modernization has brought improvement—the industries on the reservation are very successful, but the Indians have chosen to abandon the old ways entirely.

The Coeur d'Alene Reservation was established a quarter of a century after the tribe's early contact with white men. The first to come were the "Black Robes," Jesuit priests, and they were welcomed by the Coeur d'Alenes. In 1842, a Jesuit missionary was sent to live with them, and a temporary log cabin mission was built on a site where the Spokane River empties out of Lake Coeur d'Alene. A reservation was established in 1867, but much land was lost through the years to the whites, so that now the reservation consists of only 68,000 acres, of which about 13,000 is owned by the tribe as a whole.

The tribe today still reflects the early years of contact with the Jesuits for 100 percent are Catholic. Of the 900 tribal members, about half live on the reservation, and of these, half work on the reservation. Some work in the sawmills, some farm, some are road builders, some are teachers, nurses, carpenters, and auto mechanics. One is a doctor.

Only a few Indians farm since most of them are too poor to buy the equipment needed for successful large-scale farming.

In spite of the profitable industries on the reservation, and the tribal investment in industries off the reservation (a plywood plant, a planer plant, and others), the annual income is only a modest $2,500.

Actual living conditions sometimes seem poorer than that. The majority of the older homes are without running water and indoor plumbing. These houses were built in the late 1800's and early 1900's, mainly on individual lots, and are not within reach of electricity. New houses are under way, but the progress is slow.

The general health of the tribe is fair. There is a federal Indian Health Service, furnishing two clinics with three doctors each, and a hospital in St. Maries.

Educational opportunities are quite good; secondary education, at least, is available for those who wish to take advantage of it. There are three high schools within the reservation, and four grammar schools; one of them is the mission school at De Smet, which has been educating the Coeur d'Alene Indians for ninety years.

Thus, for this tribe the problems are not, with the exception of housing, basically physical. They are instead juvenile behavior and alcoholism—problems which beset much of our modern society, whether white or Indian. In adapting the white man's technology, some of the tribes, such as the Coeur d'Alene, have found that modernization has brought along the negative factors which also beset white society. Now the Coeur d'Alenes are working to combat juvenile delinquency and alcoholism.

They are obtaining juvenile officers. They are constructing a community building, gym, and swimming pool, and are trying to build a better recreational program for the younger members of the tribe. These moves, they hope, will help prevent alcoholism in the younger age group. For the adults, tribal leaders are attending workshops and conferences on the subject, held by different agencies, to learn how to decrease alcoholism on the reservation.

High income or low, this tribe finds social problems more pressing than economic ones. The Coeur d'Alenes speak of "bettering their welfare," and they speak also of "social justice." Perhaps their main concern for the future can be said to be that of many tribes: they want to retain their special relationship with the federal government, and fear termination. Because of new government policies, termination should no longer frighten the Indians, but unfortunately because of past history, it still appears as an ever-present threat to many tribes.

Some Indian projects on the reservations are vast in concept, and need huge financial assistance from both the tribe and the government. Other projects are very modest, but extremely significant, culturally and financially.

On the Fort Hall Reservation, in the southeast corner of Idaho, the Indians of the Bannock Creek District found that by their own initiative and effort they could solve a small problem that in turn extracted them "from the pit of poverty and wasted lives in which they have been mired for so long."

The Bannock Creek District is very poor and isolated from the rest of the reservation. In the beginning there was only one house that had its own well; water for the other families had to be brought from non-Indian neighbors, or from the creek which flows through the valley. Later, a half-dozen new houses were built, each with its own well. During the summer the male members of the families worked for farmers and ranchers in the area, but when winter came they were unable to find work, and subsisted on welfare.

Many of the Indians owned cars that were in such disrepair that they could not afford to have them fixed to meet the state's safety inspection standards, therefore, the people could not get safety inspection tickets. A series of meetings were held. The Indians studied their resources; there was a vacant garage, and there were two Indians who had mechanical knowledge and experience. The Bureau of Indian Affairs officials at the Fort Hall agency suggested a tribal garage. The men were asked if they would like to work for the welfare money they were getting and at the same time gain training and experience. They were responsive to the plan. A call went out for tools. A broken-down pickup truck was obtained from the tribal council, parts were purchased, and the truck was repaired, to be used to tow cars into the garage.

The men worked long hours, longer than required because they were enthusiastic about the new venture. Although the garage was poorly outfitted in the way of equipment and lacked many necessary tools, in a year it was a success: all the cars the men repaired passed inspection.

The garage was a start in the Bannock Creek District, and it is a symbol of the hope that sustains the Indians, at a time when so many have so little else.

8

THE INDIANS
OF MONTANA
AND WYOMING

Land, and the use of that land, is a key factor in the economic well-being of the Indians of Montana and Wyoming. Relatively speaking, the reservations in these states are large in acreage. However, the critics of white treatment of the Indians, and the Indians themselves, would point out that these lands are only a small part of the original Indian lands. This is a true assessment for here as in all the other states, over the years Indian land was chipped away, through seizure, homesteading, allotment, and sale. One exception is the Rocky Boy's Reservation in the northern part of Montana. (Rocky Boy was the name of a leader of a wandering band of Chippewa Indians.) This reservation is an oddity in the almost universal story of diminishing Indian lands. Today this reservation is almost double its original size.

During the nineteenth century, the Chippewas and the Crees, having no land of their own, roamed from place to place in Montana. At one time they were deported by the federal government to Canada but they managed to return. Their desperate situation was finally officially recognized, and in 1916, the Rocky Boy's Reservation of 55,000 acres was established as a refuge for the "homeless and wandering Indians of Montana." Today the reservation has over 100,000 acres.

Here the Chippewa and the Cree tribes lived and intermarried, so they are known as the Chippewa–Cree. Their land in the Bear Paw Mountains is beautiful, but remote. Some is forest, and some is open for grazing and dry farming, and there is even a small irrigated area. The Indians raise cattle, but that is limited because of the mountainous nature of the region. The problem soon seen by the people was how, then, could this land be most profitably used for more than just subsistence? All of Rocky Boy's land is tribally owned, but each Indian family has free use of 160 acres of the tribal land.

The first step of the Chippewa–Cree in their rehabilitation program was to take advantage of the natural beauty of the reservation and develop recreational facilities. They established a number of picnic and campgrounds in the mountains, and started a "recreation complex." This complex, when finished, will offer a pay campground, a motel, lodge, hunting reserves, and a ski area.

Today these Indians live as do most tribes. Some are at poverty level and depend mainly on public assistance for their living. Others are adequately employed. Yet the average annual income is only $2,800, and one wonders how these Indians, like many others, can live with so little actual cash. Yet, according to a missionary who works with them, the families are very close and are quite happy. The biggest problem is not economic, it is concern with education and social adjustment. Although on the surface it appears that most of these Indians live very much like the members of non-Indian communities, here again, is the conflict that results from living in two worlds. These Indians still want to live as Indians, and yet know they must come to terms with the white man's culture and society.

The Chippewa–Cree live in substandard housing, clustered into little communities, scattered here and there on the reservation, or isolated in various coulees and on side roads hundreds of acres from other Indians. They have been living in old log houses obtained from an abandoned government camp and moved onto the reservation. Today only fifty-one families live in modern houses, built by government-subsidized programs.

Many of the Indians are employed by the government agencies on the reservation. Some work for the Bureau of Indian Affairs on road crews, others work for the Public Health Service or in the Office of Economic Opportunity work programs on the reservation. A number find summertime employment on nearby farms or in construction in other areas of the state.

Most families own a car since it would be impossible to get to town for supplies without one. On the reservation there is one small grocery store and two gas stations. The children ride buses to school. Occasionally, there are Indian teachers, but most of them are white. The elementary school at the BIA agency is almost all Indian with a few white pupils, usually the children of some of the teachers, and in the Box Elder elementary and high schools, the students are about 80 percent Indian. Little or no Indian culture is taught to these children, but there are some sporadic attempts at teaching Indian history. The Indians are achieving something that many Indians elsewhere are still striving for: the setting up of an independent school district with an Indian school board.

This group of Chippewa–Cree is fortunate in that it has taken steps to control and direct the education of its children, and if this pattern is any indication of the future, these Indians will be aggressive about the determination of other programs, which is, after all, as it should be.

The Indians on Rocky Boy's Reservation seem to live as any rural American family does. They make family excursions to town to do the laundry in the coin-operated machines in Havre. They read and watch television. The young people go to the mission youth center to listen to records, play Ping-Pong, or watch television shows. Many adults attend hobby groups, learning to make ceramics and do fabric painting, or attend adult education programs. The men go hunting and fishing in the mountains. One difference is that, as with many Indians, hunting and fishing still provide needed food and are not simply recreational.

Perhaps the Indian culture is retained most in the language, foods, and crafts. Some of the families use their language, Cree, at home, although many others speak it but do not use it consistently. Nearly everyone understands English.

Although food preparation is not too different from that of the nearby white families, some Indian foods are in common use. Among them are grease bread, biscuit dough rolled out and fried in deep fat, and bannock, a baked biscuit dough. Another typical Indian food that is fairly common is dried meat, or jerky, usually made from venison. This is sometimes eaten for a snack or pounded up with chokecherries or June berries (service berries) to make pemmican. Most of the families rely heavily on deer for their meat, although they also buy beef in the butcher shop.

The crafts still practiced include the making of moccasins, beadwork, ties, and the tanning of hides. There is a cooperative organization of the Indians that markets the crafts, which are sold through an outlet in a restaurant in Box Elder, and at the various trading posts.

According to a non-Indian observer on the reservation, these Chippewa–Cree Indians seem to be quite happy; they also indicate clearly that they want to retain their identity as a people, if not their culture, and to be left alone to determine their own future. They have, for the most part, successfully adjusted to the white man's society, but they *are* Indians and want to continue to be.

Another group of Indians who live in a scenic area where the beauty of the land will be economic salvation, if it can be successfully exploited, are those on the Flathead Reservation in the Rocky Mountains. Within the reservation is Flathead Lake, surrounded by mountains, forests, and streams. This reservation, unlike many, is not an island of poor people in a stream of plenty, but rather an integral part of the area around it.

The Flatheads who came to the land long ago consisted of the Salish and Kootanai Indian tribes. The Salish had been dubbed Flathead by the coastal Indians to the west, not because they had flat heads, but on the contrary, because their heads were normal, whereas some of the coastal tribes practiced head distortion.

These Salish and Kootanai, from the first contact with the early fur traders, trappers, and settlers, intermarried with the whites, and also with one another, an integration that has continued to the present. Today although about half the tribal members live on the reservation, the majority of residents are not Indians.

These non-Indians, unfortunately, own most of the land that is suitable for farming within the reservation. The remaining valley land suitable for either crops or grazing consists of farm units too small to make profitable use of large-scale mechanized farm methods. In addition, the land has risen in value so much that farm returns are not great enough to justify using the land for that purpose.

The Indians feel that their best course of development is in recreational and retirement areas, and many observers agree. There is great natural beauty in the area, the climate is good for at least three seasons of the year, and the population is so low that there is room for expansion. In addition to the lake, there are streams and pure underground water. Electric power is now ample and could be expanded, since it is supplied from Montana's Kerr Dam, located on a site leased by the tribes.

The tribes have recognized this recreational potential and they operate a resort facility at Blue Bay on the eastern shore of Flathead Lake, and a bathhouse at Hot Springs. Further development could increase the tribal income, as could the development of a number of excellent hydroelectric dam sites on the Flathead River, within the reservation. Some income for the tribes today comes from a commercial timber industry, which could also be expanded.

The individuals of the tribes are better educated, more integrated, and more self-sufficient than those on most reservations. Their tribal government continues to plan for future improvements. A credit program exists, which allows members to borrow money to start businesses, build homes, or further their education. With such financial backing, the progress of individual Indians will be determined by his own initiative and willingness to work.

According to a BIA official, the problems on the Flathead Reservation are not economic or the obtaining of minimum necessities, but rather, emotional. Here crops up, as it does with many Indian tribes, the comment about "identity." Fully three-quarters of these Indians have established a "tribal identity" and take pride in their ancestry and are secure in their acceptance by the total community. But, as one BIA official said, "for that fraction of the Indian population so affected, the basic problem is the establishment of identity and the understanding that they will be accepted by the whole community for what they are and do as individuals." Anger and criticism of whites is not usually directed toward matters of physical well-being. The resentment occurs, and is mainly among the younger Indians, as a BIA official said, because "like every other member of the human race, they need a sense of identity, of importance and of belonging. Indian people need and deserve full and unpatronizing acceptance of themselves for what they are— intelligent, talented and warmhearted people who have had to live with a staggering burden of handicaps to establishment of an identity they could take pride in."

The use of land on another of Montana's reservations presents different problems. The Fort Peck Reservation of the Assiniboine and Sioux, in the northeast corner of the state, consists of over 2 million acres of prairie land and embraces the broad flood plain of the Missouri River, which forms the southern border of the reservation, and many valleys with streams and rivers. This farmland is good land. Unfortunately the Indians own less than half the reservation, and there are twice as many white people on the land as there are Indians.

The Indians here, then, are faced with the problem of what use to make of the land that they do own, to take care of their 4,000 residents, and to build up the tribe economically.

The timber—cottonwood, ash, willow and box elder—has

little commercial value, but it is used for shelter for livestock and game, corral posts, and for firewood. There are wild fruits and berries, such as chokecherries, June berries, bull berries and currants. These are gathered by the Indians and make up an important, if not a large part, of their diet along with wild turnips, dried game and corn.

About half of the Indian land is under cultivation, with wheat, barley and safflower. There is grazing land, dry farmland, and irrigated farmland, but this land is being lost to the Indians at a rate of 5,000 acres per year through sales to non-Indians. These Indians have an agricultural economy, which has been good for some and bad for others. There is a tremendous range of conditions in the same area. Some Indian families are well-to-do farmers and ranchers; others are unbelievably poor.

In spite of the number of very successful farmers, there are many more unskilled men who depend on seasonal agricultural or construction work for a living. There has been a great problem of unemployment, and more than half the Indian families live on less than $3,000 per year, and many of them live on much less.

In addition to the low income and large-scale unemployment (between 45 and 80 percent), the problems are substandard housing, malnutrition, lack of sanitation facilities and crowded home conditions.

As of a survey a few years ago, only 48 percent of the Indian homes were classified as being in a good condition, 19 percent were in fair condition, and 33 percent were in poor condition. And 14 percent of the homes had two or more families living in one house. The latest survey of conditions inside the houses showed that only 50 percent had electricity. Only 23 percent had a telephone, 81 percent had a radio, and 71 percent had television.

The poor housing conditions have caused a high rate of sickness and infant mortality from diarrhea, dysentery and pneumonia. It is hard to pinpoint any one answer to why these conditions exist—and, of course, they do not exist for all the members of the tribe.

As a whole the tribal members are better educated than many tribes, and are well versed in the ways of the white man. Individually, the range is great—there are people of great political sophistication, and others who are totally lacking in education. Generally, the average number of school years completed by the Indian population varies between 6.5 and 10.6 years.

It is most obvious that these Indians need more houses and more jobs. According to a BIA official, they also need better opinions of themselves, greater opportunities for self-expression and self-determination, and respect from others.

The tribal leaders are all too aware of the problems of their peoples. The land belonging to the Indians is not providing sufficient employment or income. Their answer has been to try to persuade industries to come to the reservation. For years these leaders have sought this in vain, for the reservation is isolated, far from markets and raw materials, and has a cold climate. Recently the leaders decided on a crash program to help themselves. Within a six-month period they planned and established the Fort Peck Tribal Industries—an organization solely owned by the tribes—and quickly went into operation, signing a management contract with the Dynalectron Corporation, a plant that overhauls rifles for the United States Government.

It probably is not possible for a non-Indian, not living on the

Fort Peck Tribal Industries, Poplar, Montana

Head Start class on the Fort Peck Reservation, Poplar, Montana

reservation, to understand the uplift this project gave to these Indians. William Youpee, chairman of the tribal executive board, radiated excitement when he spoke before the U.S. House of Representatives Committee on Education and Labor. He called the development the "most important economic event that has happened on the Fort Peck Reservation in many years." Here at last was an industry which believed that the Indians could do the job. And the federal government was showing the same confidence in the Indians by awarding the contract for work. Here was the chance the Indians had been waiting for—to show that they could function well in the white man's industrial society.

At about the same time that this venture was successfully launched by the tribe, a new housing manufacturing plant was built on the tribe's new industrial park. Unemployment went down. It had been 47 percent, now it was 37 percent. As Mr. Youpee pointed out to the House Committee, the 10 percent reduction does not sound like much, but it meant a tremendous amount to the Fort Peck Indians. "There was a new feeling," Mr. Youpee said, that "perhaps, after all, we could do something to improve things here."

"Things," aside from the industries, are progressing. Houses are being built and improved. A motel is on the drawing board, as is an arts and crafts center. There are sanitation improvement programs, community action programs, Head Start, Job Corps, Vista, legal services—many projects are under way to make a better life for the Indians.

One cannot say that the Fort Peck Indians found the transition from an agricultural economy to a more industrialized situation difficult because they retained much of their Indian ways, although for a non-Indian there would be a tendency to

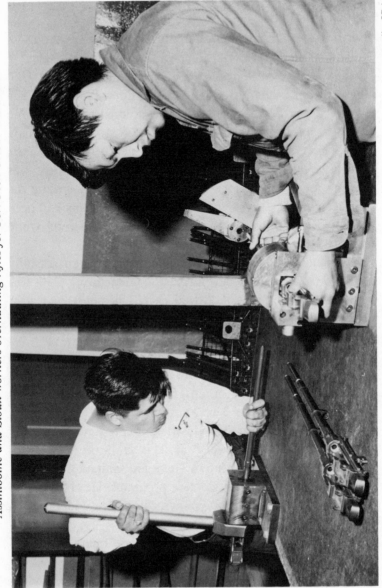

Assiniboine and Sioux workers overhauling rifles for Fort Peck Tribal Industries

credit: SBA

jump to that conclusion. But it has been shown, by tribe after tribe, that there is no need to lose the Indian culture by adopting the white man's industrial know-how. Many tribes have successfully kept their identity, their culture, their pride in their "Indian-ness," and still have been able to progress economically. As a matter of fact, many of the Assiniboine and Sioux speak often of the need and desire to keep the best of their culture, and to accept the best of the white man's. These Assiniboine and Sioux on Fort Peck have kept much of their own ways. The family is an extremely strong unit, and generally is an extended unit, with the immediate family sharing with its relatives. They still prepare foods similar to those prepared in the past, and they have Indian celebrations often, as well as a very modern three-day rodeo.

These Indians are extremely talented in their arts and crafts. They make all kinds of beaded articles, including medallions, earrings, purses, ties, belts, and moccasins. They also make articles for their dancing costumes, including war bonnets and porcupine headdresses. One of the craft items that is well known is the star quilt, which the Indian women were originally taught to make by the missionaries.

With so much stress on retaining the skills and the customs of the past, it is easy to see that these Indians will keep a good part of their culture for some time to come. Here, the major problem seems to be improving economic and physical conditions, so that the customs can be enjoyed in an atmosphere of well-being.

The Fort Peck Indians found that they needed to bring industry to the land, but for the Northern Cheyenne Indians, who are on a reservation in the southeastern part of the state, the

Albert Magpie, Northern Cheyenne Indian

land itself is the prime factor in the economic picture in a different way from the others mentioned before.

The Northern Cheyenne, who call themselves the Morning Star People, a name taken from one of their famed leaders of the last century, live on a reservation of about 440,000 acres in a rugged semi-mountainous area. Luckily the tribe still owns most of the land. The land is valuable, not in the same sense as the land of Indians in Palm Springs or Tacoma, but because it has brought a good income to the Indians. It is suitable primarily for livestock grazing, and up until only a few years ago, the main source of income for the tribal government was the grazing fees paid by individual stockmen, or by the tribal steer-raising enterprise (which was liquidated in 1969). But now the land is promising much more. Oil companies have become interested in the reservation, and in one year they paid the tribe more than $1 million for leasing about 134,000 acres, in addition to the money they paid in annual exploratory rental. There has not been an oil discovery to date on the reservation, but there must be promise for the companies to persist so. Also, in the past few years a major coal company has been exploring the reservation, and it seems likely that a coal mine will be opened in this decade. Fortunately, the mineral rights are held by the tribal government, not by individuals, so the increased income to the tribe will allow it to expand its aid programs for members.

The tribe as a group has good assets. In addition it has sought and received aid, financial and otherwise, from various departments of the federal government to initiate and carry out many projects—schools, road construction, range conservation, employment assistance, health service, and housing.

A great boost was given to the tribe's housing situation when

Teacher and children in a Head Start program on the Lame Deer Reservation, Montana

credit: BIA

several years ago the tribe was awarded $3.9 million as a settlement of its old claims against the federal government. Through this settlement the tribe was able to give each member $1,000 to be spent for "family improvement." Much of this "family plan" money was used for building and remodeling homes. Also ninety-five mobile homes were purchased. The result is that today most Northern Cheyenne families are adequately housed.

The progress these Indians have made as a tribe is remarkable when one realizes that for years, because of their location in this rugged semimountainous area, they had been largely isolated from contact with non-Indians. It was only fifteen years ago that the first paved highway was built across the reservation. Today Lame Deer, the reservation headquarters, is still forty-five miles from the nearest railroad or bus station. It is also remarkable that the average income of the Northern Cheyennes is greater than that of most of the other Indian tribes on reservations, yet it is still less than one-third of the state or national averages. Within the tribe there are great differences in income; some of the families, usually families with two wage earners, have incomes of over $10,000 a year. A far greater number have no visible source of income at all, other than welfare, and a third or more of all families receive some welfare assistance during the course of a year.

About a fifth of these Cheyennes live in rural areas, along the streams and rivers, and it is among these that the earning of cash income is most difficult. Most of the Indians are concentrated in four communities, where they work for corporations such as one which manufactures plastic items and costume jewelry, or for the St. Labre Indian Mission, which operates a school. Many of the tribal members work for the federal gov-

Northern Cheyenne Indians employed by Guild Arts and Crafts, Ashland, Montana

credit: BIA

ernment; more than 60 percent of all federal employees on the reservation are Indians.

It can be seen that this tribe is relatively stable economically, and the members are better off financially than those of many other tribes. The outstanding difficulties today seem to be based on attitude, or past conditioning. Too often the Indian parents are uninterested or distrustful of education for their children. Thus the children are not encouraged, and their educational level is below average. This starts off a chain reaction, for without sufficient education, employment is difficult, and the lack of that employment not only results in a lack of money, but is discouraging to the people. This discouragement and resultant lack of self-confidence has another effect, for it makes it difficult for individual Indians to leave the reservation and relocate in areas where there are greater job opportunities. Those who become distressed about their situations turn to alcohol for solace, and there is a definite excessive use of alcohol on the reservation. Perhaps, as one BIA official commented, "only time can solve some of the problems." As he remarked, the Indians have been asked to make more adjustments in the last 100 years than most groups have had to make in a thousand years or more.

The Wind River Reservation, Wyoming's only Indian reservation, is a prime example of another problem: the failure of the Indians to make proper use of their resources. The Indians here own land which comprises one of the best watered parts of Wyoming. The reservation is located just east of the Continental Divide; on the north are the Owl Creek Mountains and on the west, the Wind River Range. Down from these heights flow streams and rivers, forming fertile valleys and rolling plains in the lower elevations where most of the Indians live.

On the reservation live two tribes. The Shoshones were there first, and they were joined one cold winter by the Northern Arapahoes, who at the time were homeless. They were given land on the Wind River Reservation, which today totals over 2 million acres.

The Indians grow hay and small grains and over a million and a half acres are open grazing land. But these are not the greatest of the blessings: the land contains oil and gas. There are 367 productive oil wells and thirty-nine gas wells, which provide most of the tribal income—about $3 million. In addition, there are other natural resources which are being explored —phosphate deposits, coal, gypsum, bentonite, and uranium.

In addition to the good income provided by the land, the tribe has benefited from monies from the government, as a result of claims filed. A few years ago the Arapahoes received nearly $3 million in judgment funds, and currently the Shoshone tribe expects to receive more than $6 million from a claim settlement from the government.

Why then, with this income, are conditions as bad as they are on the reservation? Why are only 48 percent of the Indians employed full time? Why is the median educational level of the Indians approximately only nine years? The two tribes should have over 200 college graduates to equal the national percentage, but they have less than two dozen, in spite of the fact that both tribes have and provide scholarship monies for college attendance. There has been much physical progress on the reservation: there is an industrial park; there are community centers and housing projects. But even in the category of housing, these Indians lag. The housing is inadequate, and of the estimated 900 housing units, approximately 70 percent have deteriorated, or are too small, or both.

The tribal councils and Indians in general support such programs as range improvement, weed control, fish and game management, credit programs and road construction and improvement. And there are more job opportunities with the industries and the mineral exploitation.

It is difficult to determine why these Indians have not reached a better economic and educational level. Some feel that the tribes have not exploited fully the resources, the natural *and* the human. The land has given much to these Indians, but perhaps in its use, even more could be gained. Here is an area in which the sociologists might well help. There are none of the usual problems of tribal poverty, so there should be a good deal more progress. In fact, these Indians are better off than many whites and still do not live as well.

The Indians have not tapped many resources. They could commercialize tourist attractions on the reservation: there is the beauty of the red canyons; there are the clear lakes; and the wild flowers on the mountains next to swift running streams. Skilled craftsmen make items for sale, and there are the traditional Indian dances, held almost nightly during the summer, and sun dances and religious ceremonies held each year. There surely is much that the tourist would enjoy.

One answer: as far as the human resources are concerned, some feel that the Indians need to be inspired to grasp the opportunities offered to them. There are adequate school facilities, but the Indians must want the education and learn to respect it, for it is only with this education and training, that they can hope to benefit from the physical advances that are being made constantly on the reservation through industry and mineral development. As one economic development worker at Wind River said:

Every day the reservation waits for its own engineer, geologist and attorney puts the reservation weeks, months and perhaps years behind the rest of the country. Each time Datel (an electronics manufacturing corporation) brings in an electrical engineer, Gulf Oil hires a geologist from Texas and U.S. Steel transfers an attorney from New York, the reservation becomes more isolated behind the "diploma curtain" that separates the reservation from the economic progress of the country and the nation.

Somewhere on the reservation is tomorrow's engineer, geologist, or attorney, but tomorrow will be a long time coming unless today's children get a good education.

9

THE INDIANS OF
THE LOWER PLATEAU

The Indians of Nevada, Utah, and Colorado have long been called the lower Plateau Indians. Their ancestors probably came to the area between ten-and twenty-thousand years ago as hunters following the game trails of the bison. Today in Nevada there are fifteen reservations, and ten small colonies with a total of less than 5,000 Indians. Perhaps another 2,000 Indians live in non-Indian communities in the state. The largest reservation in Nevada is very big but it has often been cited as an example of the bad treatment of the Indians by the federal government. Pyramid Lake Reservation, thirty miles from Reno, has over 475,000 acres, a quarter of which is Pyramid Lake. This lake, deeded to the Paiute Indians in 1859, once was said to be "set like a gem in the mountains."

Its waters and banks abounded with fish and wildlife, and even a pelican rookery. Geysers and hot springs were nearby. Then in the early 1900's the federal government began to concern itself with irrigation, and the Department of Interior dammed the Truckee River just above Pyramid Lake to divert water. This was supposed to make about 287,000 dry acres suitable for farming and ranching. By 1930 the Indians realized that there were only a few trout left in the lake, since water from the river had been diverted so the trout could not swim upstream to spawn; the tribe began to take legal steps to regain the water. Thus started a long struggle. The Indians claim that the Derby Dam continues to divert more water from the river than can be used, and it is true that the level of Pyramid Lake is falling each year. Some of the diverted water goes to a duck hunting preserve, some to an area where white ranchers have a community cow pasture.

For years the Indians protested in vain. Then recently a compact was proposed between California and Nevada which would give California rights to 50,000 acre-feet of this water annually with a right to use more as the need arose. The Indians were thrust into the middle of the white fight for water. A Nevada engineer who supported the compact said that the Paiutes had no legal right to Truckee River water, even though it is the only river feeding the lake. However, in 1969, Secretary of the Interior Walter Hickel took an opposite point of view. He said that the compact "impinges upon the water rights of the Pyramid Lake tribe of Paiute Indians who own the lake."

The controversy grew. In early 1969 a *New York Times* article was headlined: "Nevada Indians Fight For a Lake." By summer of 1969 *The Washington Post* headline was: "Hickel Gets Caught in Oasis Row." Later Mr. Hickel was to change his public stand, and advocate a compromise which could not possibly benefit the Paiutes or Pyramid Lake. The Indians felt betrayed because no one would defend their right to the water. The problem here is that the Indians stand in the way of white man's "progress" and the vested interests of big capital in California are not likely to let principle win a victory over money.

Naturally enough, cases like this one of Pyramid Lake embitter the Indians, and cause justifiable criticism of a government, which today speaks apologetically about the "injustices" of the past, while continuing to perpetrate many new injustices in the name of "need."

Where the Indians do not have anything the whites want anymore, they do better. One example is the small reservation, the Yomba, with only 810 acres and fifty-three tribal members. On this isolated reservation the Indians live quite well, quietly contained, as cattle ranchers. There are no industries, yet only one person of employable age does not work. The ranchers make a good living, $300 per month, though they are the first to admit that they are not going to get rich in cattle ranching. Surprisingly, for being so very isolated, they live very much like the white ranchers, since the Indian culture as such seems to be lost to the Yomba Indians. They still practice the crafts of basket making, and rug and blanket weaving but for their own use, not for sale. Instead of learning crafts, the children go to the Yomba School on the reservation where there are two teachers for fifteen children. The Indians are little interested in any kind of white man's politics today, and very few have ever voted. This is again, undoubtedly due to the isolation, and the very poor roads on the reservation. In spite of distant health facilities—in Schurz, which is 150 miles away, and the nearest doctor thirty-five miles away in Gabbs—the tribe is healthy and has a sense of well-being.

There is another group of Indians in Nevada who have lost everything Indian: their culture and their land. They live in a colony on twenty-eight acres near the cities of Reno and Sparks.

About 600 Indians live here today, some in shacks, some in mutual self-help houses, and some in houses that were privately built. The children attend the city schools and the adults are employed in the cities, in construction, warehousing and forestry jobs. They live like the whites, and work like the whites. Their average family income is $3,220, compared to the $8,600 for the area as a whole; and yet these Indians, unlike many other Indians are not displeased. They feel that absorption in the main culture is an end in itself. They have been absorbed, and will continue to be so. Whether or not they will be integrated and properly paid is another matter.

It is easy to see when examining the Indian tribes today that there never can be an average of anything. Some farm, some ranch, some are isolated, some are urban, some are poor, some are not-so-poor, some have little land, others have much. As this is true throughout the country, it is true with these lower Plateau Indians and there are some startling examples.

In Utah today there is one tribe that is an important economic and social force in its state, with a million acres of land, $9 million in assets, and 5,000 head of cattle. These Indians are the Utes of the Uintah and Ouray Reservation.

They might be called "rich." They are lucky in that they have had a different history than many of the Indians with respect to termination. When the termination policy began, the Utes were already receiving good income from oil and gas development of their land. At about this time, in 1950, the government awarded the Uintah and Ouray Reservation 60 percent of a judgment from the federal government as a result of claims, and the tribe got more than $3.1 million. With these funds, and the healthy income from the oil and gas development, some Utes (especially those of mixed blood) asked to be terminated from federal supervision. But not all Utes felt that way. The result was the Ute Partition Act of 1954, which formally separated the two groups, and by 1961 federal supervision was terminated over the activities of those mixed-blood Utes who wished to withdraw. (There are 490 of these mixed-blood members of the Ute tribe who still generally reside in the area but receive no services provided for Indians.) The remaining Ute Indians in the tribe occupy land which is mainly held by the tribe (which operates as a corporation), or by individual Indians as allotted land.

The tribe is engaged in big business: it not only operates the largest cattle herd in the state, but oversees a very complicated budget, and manages tremendous acreages of land within the eastern part of Utah which includes mineral deposits and oil. The tribe also runs its own irrigation system, has developed its own recreation program, and through its Public Housing Authority (which is controlled jointly by the Ute tribe, Bureau of Indian Affairs, and non-Indians in the locality), it expects to provide adequate housing for all Ute Indians by 1974.

The Utes, unlike many Indian tribes, have had the advice, or the "know-how," to make use of the financial assistance offered by many federal government agencies. They have had the help the Wind River Indians need. Here is how it worked: a grant from the Office of Economic Opportunity, and the technical assistance of the Bureau of Indian Affairs and the University of Utah helped the tribe start the Ute Fabricating Company, which produces quality furniture with artistic Indian designs, for schools, motels, and so on. It has been a tremendously successful venture.

Then, the tribe applied to the Economic Development Administration for money to build a tribal complex, which will eventually include a motel, restaurant, boat marina and service station. And perhaps, even more important, the tribe was able to get a federal grant for monies to train Indians to manage this complex.

Here is a tribe that is interested, eager, and willing to seek aid, so that it can progress with projects that will better its own economic, educational and social conditions. For today, compared with other Indians, the condition of the Uintah and Ouray Utes could be called superb. Most of the Utes live in houses with running water, electricity and all modern conveniences. Although there is some unemployment, the Utes have gas resources which will bring in more industry to provide jobs.

The problem that looms largest to these Indians has nothing to do with economics or minimal standards of living. It is the question of education. And here it is a question of quality: Ute youngsters who attend public schools (and most of them do) are not being educated as well as their fellow non-Indian students. An alarmingly large percentage of the Ute students are unable to read, write or speak effectively after having attended nine years of public school. This situation bodes ill for the future— how can the tribe then have effective leadership to administer the Ute tribal affairs? The tribal leaders hope that the attitude of the non-Indians and the non-Indian teachers toward the Indians will change for the better, and that they will expect more, and give more, to these students. Another part of the problem is the need for a more respectful attitude toward white man's education by both Indian students and parents. Attempts are being made by both the Utes and non-Indians who work directly with them to bring about these changes in attitude, but until they succeed, the difficulties will remain essentially as they are.

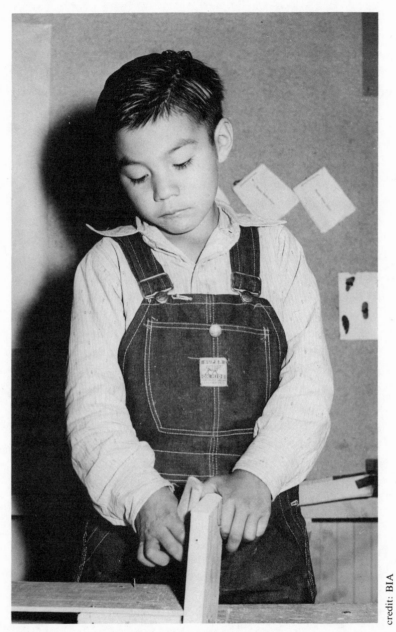

Ute boy in arts and crafts class

credit: BIA

These Utes are economically successful, in direct contrast to the approximately 1,000 Colorado Utes who live on the Ute Mountain Ute Reservation. These Indians live in what is called the Four-Corners area—the meeting point of the four states of Colorado, New Mexico, Utah and Arizona. It has been said of them that, "these Colorado Utes have often been forgotten when Americans have considered Indians and Indian problems. These fine people have often lived with frustration, lack of understanding and lack of consideration."

As far back as the 1940's these Utes have had frightful financial problems, with few job opportunities, little family income, and insufficient returns from the rangelands. Even today the majority of the tribal members could be rated only from poor to fair as far as economic well-being and self-sufficiency are concerned.

These Utes lived so poorly and had so little money through the years that the tribe as a whole supported nearly all of its people. Any money that came in to the tribe, such as a sum they received after World War II (with expansion of oil and gas development in the area), and monies received from the federal government from claims, went to support the day-to-day living of the Indians. Because the tribe took care of its own, the Indians developed neither job skills, nor the desire to acquire any. Here was dependency, not on the federal government, as with so many Indian tribes, but upon the tribe itself.

When the Bureau of Indian Affairs finally devoted an agency to the reservation in 1968, for the sole purpose of helping only that reservation, the pattern was set, and it caused great disagreement and much friction. The Bureau, as advisor, felt that the tribal money should be spent on development of the reservation, on projects that would help the Indians get on a firm economic footing, not by doling out monies to the tribal members. Money coming in from oil and gas was money gained from "depleting assets," that is, natural assets that, once used, were gone forever. The Indians had to see that supporting its members daily would not leave anything on which to build for the future.

Now a new start has been made. Land has been cleared, so that a cattle enterprise can be successful. Streets are being paved and gutters put in; housing is being built; water and sanitation projects are under way. Certain of the Indians are voluntarily taking job training; education is being expanded. Efforts are being made to attract industry. It is good that a start has been made, for it has been estimated that if the past situation continued, the Indians would, within six years, find themselves living in a community *nearly totally dependent on welfare payments*. The Indians on this reservation are suffering the pangs of change. According to one BIA official, he can see only "traumatic and confusing days ahead for members of the older generation. We see them resisting loss of the 'old way' and conflicts between them and their children. . . . We see days of turmoil followed by sound growth." Yet this growth will be a long time coming: an estimate of twenty-five years to reach local self-sufficiency for the Colorado Utes.

10

THE INDIANS
OF THE DAKOTAS

The Indians of the Dakotas today may be among the most miserable in America. Some of the tribes have assets as tribes, but the income, the money the individual Indian family has for food, clothing and all necessities, is sickeningly low in this generally affluent society of ours. Take the case of the Indians at Fort Berthold Reservation in western North Dakota. The average income for a family of four is about $1,800 a year.

There are no towns on the reservation. Eighty percent of the Indians are unemployed. There are no U.S. highways on the reservation and the roads are gravel; there are no buses. Telephone service is limited. Housing is poor; most of the homes could be classed as substandard because of their deteriorating condition, lack of utilities and sanitary facilities. Alcoholism and juvenile problems are high. There is no community development spirit. The Indians lack confidence in their abilities. They lack long range plans or objectives. They "live a day by day existence without consideration of the future. . . . They have strong feelings over what the white man has done or is doing to or for the Indian people. They do not trust the federal government. . . ."

Long ago these Indians, the Arikara, Mandan, and Gros Ventre, banded together for mutual protection from raiding and hostile Sioux. These tribes, called the Three Affiliated Tribes, were joined on a single reservation in 1851. Cholera epidemics, raids, smallpox—all took their toll. And consistently, too, parts of the reservation were lost as a right-of-way to the gold fields and to the military. There were unsuccessful efforts to move the Indians to Oklahoma toward the end of the nineteenth century when the government decided that the Fort Berthold lands were unproductive. Then the government took more land without the consent of the three tribes for the Northern Pacific Railway. White homesteading took more in the 1880's and in 1910 another big chunk was ceded. It was in the 1950's, however, that the biggest blow was dealt to this reservation. At that time a great government reclamation project, the Garrison Dam, was completed, and this dam caused the flooding of 155,000 acres of the best agricultural lands of the reservation. The large reservoir that resulted was named Lake Sakakawea, and now divides the reservation into five distinct segments. Needless to say, Garrison Dam was not built for the benefit of the Indians.

The tribes were paid about $5 million for the land; the money was deposited to the credit of the tribes. An additional appropriation of $7.5 million was authorized for credit to the tribes for intangible damages from taking the land.

But it was small compensation for the tremendous hardship that resulted. Ninety percent of the Indians lived in this lush farmland in the Missouri Valley, where there were springs and creeks for water, exposed coal beds for fuel supply and plenty of wood. There were wild fruits and game with which to supplement the food supply. With the coming of the Garrison Dam these people were moved, but instead of moving whole villages, each family's home was moved to its allotment in the highlands. Here the land was mainly suited to ranching. Relocation destroyed any semblance of organization; families were separated, and often by great distances, since the lake cut the land into five segments, with no bridges on the reservation. The segments are totally isolated one from another. To go one mile across the reservoir, one may have to drive a hundred miles. (Eighty percent of the road system in the area was taken for the reservoir.)

Today, after the government wrecked their reservation, many groups are trying to help these Indians. Welfare—and the number of persons receiving assistance has steadily increased since relocation days—is provided either by the counties or the Bureau of Indian Affairs. The latter agency would like to help these Indians get on their feet, but as one official said, budget restrictions have slowed or brought some of the Bureau programs to a halt. The employment assistance program is at a standstill because no funds are available to send people out for employment or training. No funds are available to conduct on-the-job training programs on the reservation.

The land must be developed by range improvement and irrigation, yet the total land suitable for agriculture would only support about a third of the Indian population if it were used properly. Minerals could be developed. It is estimated, for example, that the reservation contains one of the largest deposits of lignite (coal) in the world, and yet no development of this has been started, because the tribe and the Bureau are without funds to provide for mapping the appropriate areas. There are twenty-six producing oil wells on the reservation, but further exploration is needed. Again, there are no funds available for this.

One of the few bright spots in reservation living is the educational picture. There are three new schools, and forty-nine students attend colleges and universities throughout the country. Fifty percent of the high school graduates attend colleges, and 50 percent go to vocational schools. So at least these Indians seem to have the belief in education, which will, in due time, help them solve their many problems.

Several other tribes in North Dakota have dreadfully low individual incomes. Among the Chippewa Indians who live on the Turtle Mountain Reservation, near the Canadian border, the average family income is about $1,972 per year and again this low income is coupled with a high unemployment rate. Thirty-six percent of the employable adults are unemployed; there is no work for them. Almost 2,000 persons a month receive welfare assistance at an average cost of $70,566 per month. It would seem there must be a better way to help these Indians. The tribe receives very little income from land leased primarily to Indians on the reservation and adjacent to it. But this is the only source of income for the tribe as a whole, and without adequate funds, it is difficult for the Indians to develop the reservation. There is some good timber, and there are berries which could be of use commercially. The Indians have tried to attract industry to the reservation to provide jobs, but manufacturers have been loath to go to this distant, rugged, wooded land. Until the unemployment situation can be solved somehow, the Indians will have to tolerate these conditions. The hope for better living conditions in the near future is not great.

South Dakota has many more Indian reservations than does North Dakota, but here too, most of the Indians live under very poor conditions. Straddling both South Dakota and North Dakota is the Standing Rock Reservation of 850,000 acres (originally it was 2,332,483) where about 4,500 Indians live. Conditions here are very bad compared to much of the white society. Some of the Indians live in "communities" which are miles apart out in the country; other Indian homes are scattered throughout the reservation. But no matter the exact location, the houses are fairly uniform in style: only 25 percent of them have complete sanitation facilities. There is an inadequate running water supply and only about 30 percent of the homes have electricity. Thus, it can be seen, housing needs to be greatly improved. The rate of unemployment needs to be lowered, too, for the past several years, it has ranged around 65 percent. Yet, these Indians, living under difficult conditions, are really trying to plan for a decent future. Nobody knows why, but they are not thoroughly disheartened. They are working with spark and enthusiasm. The Standing Rock Sioux Tribe has published a very attractive brochure inviting industry to locate on the reservation: "Our future lies in the hands of industrial economics and human resources development."

These Indians know that they must bring industry to the reservation to provide jobs and think they can. They are trying hard, and perhaps industry will come. They have the Oahe Reservoir on the east boundary, which can provide water and power. The reservation has a good transportation system, consisting of railroads, federal and state highways, country roads, Indian service roads, and even landing strips for light non-commercial aircraft.

Along with the development of industry, the tribe is looking toward the development of recreational facilities to boost the economy. They have already developed some areas—a park which has rodeo grounds, a grandstand, a racetrack and horse chutes, and places for powwows and camping. Other parks which have other facilities, using the great possibilities offered by the Oahe Reservoir, are in the planning stage.

So here is the heartening situation of Indians personally living in miserable conditions, who are undaunted, and are striving, with very little help.

Those fortunate Indians whose tribes have good financial assets, obviously have more hope that their personal situations will improve. For if a tribe has money, it can develop programs, either exploit the land, or develop facilities so industry will want to come to the reservation, or build new housing.

This is most certainly the case of the Cheyenne River Indians, who have a reservation bordering that of the Standing Rock Sioux. These 4,000 Indians live on over two and a half million acres and the tribe as a whole has assets of $24 million. This tribe has gone into the business world in a big way, with investments in a Super-Value store, a garage and filling station, a laundromat, a beef camp, and the only telephone franchise awarded to an Indian tribe in the United States. This telephone company is most successful; when the tribe took it over in 1958, it had roughly 400 subscribers. Today it has 1,039 customers and assets of $778,000. Tribal officials say it makes a "good profit."

All of this, yet the individual income of the average Indian family of this tribe is around $1,500 per year. Unemployment is high here, too, for 68 percent of the Indians are without jobs. There is little industry on the reservation to provide the needed jobs. Nearby, off the reservation are coal mines and other industries which provide some, but not much, employment for the Indians. Requests have been made to the federal government for aid to help establish industries on the reservation, but with no success. The raising of livestock, and some grain farming are the main sources of income and jobs.

It stands to reason that although the individual Indians lack economic well-being, they will eventually have more jobs and better pay if the tribe continues to use its money to develop the reservation. How long this will take one cannot estimate. What they need is developmental help which almost certainly must come from the government.

This pattern of high tribal assets but poor individual income is repeated again on the Lower Brule Reservation, which is in the center of South Dakota. Here the tribal assets are not as great as with the Cheyenne River Indians (only $1.5 million), yet the individual incomes are almost double. Seventy-nine percent of the Indian families have incomes of less than $3,000, but on this reservation there is industry, and the tribal leaders have been successful in making use of the various federal government agencies to help them.

One such industry, the Iron Nation Corporation, started operations on the reservation early in 1970, and is proving to be a great success. It was formed between the tribe and white businessmen in Sioux Falls, and the plant now makes U.S. mail bags under contract to the government. With the help of the Economic Development Administration, an industrial park was built, to which the tribe hopes to attract more industries.

The Lower Brule Reservation which consists of rolling grass hills and flat land, borders on the Big Bend Reservoir, and here again is the story of the federal government changing the natural environment of an Indian reservation. In 1963 the government built the Big Bend Dam on the Missouri, and old Lower Brule was all under water. But in this case the change proved to be a blessing: the tribe received over $2 million in settlement for the lands lost to the reservoir by the building of the dam, and these monies were invested in various tribal programs, such as community development, ranching and farming, education and land purchase. Some of the funds became available for the individual Indians to borrow to enlarge their farm or ranch operations.

Homes had to be moved as a result of the dam construction, but this, too, had its compensations. As one Indian mother said, "we lost all our trees, we had to move our homes and everyone that had land in the 'taking area' received money for the value lost. We had new homes built for us in the new townsite, running water was supplied, which we never had before, and most of us had electric lights for the first time and oil heaters." So, here the Indian situation was improved by the move to new lands.

Of course, there are problems today on the reservation—it would be hard to find a reservation without them. With the Lower Brule tribe, there is unemployment, about 45 percent, but that is dramatically less than on some of the other South Dakota reservations. There is a drinking problem, but this is recognized, and the tribe has recently provided recreational activities for both the youth and the adults. A teen center has been started, and an adult recreation center has been opened where the Indians can play pool and cards. And there are dances, basketball games, roller skating, and rodeos. These tribal projects are greatly helped by the church groups who are very active in these programs.

An Indian family on the Lower Brule lives very much like

the white families nearby. They dress the same, their menus are very much the same, their youngsters swim, hike, bowl, play basketball, and prefer long hair like the white children. In one family, the boys have two horses, and the family has two dogs and one black cat, Ebony. The family watches television, and has a fairly new car. The husband is a truck driver for the Bureau of Indian Affairs, and is a skilled mechanic, trained at a school in North Dakota. This family is now planning to secure a small business loan and open a garage and filling station on the reservation.

As many white mothers, the Indian woman of this family works for the church auxiliary, and her children all go to Sunday school. Much of the daily living seems so very similar to that of a white family, yet the "Indian-ness" remains, in the language, which is spoken now only by a few, and in the dances which are enjoyed by all. The family's daughter goes to the movies, but she also dances the traditional dances in a costume made by her grandmother who is known for her beautiful beadwork. So the old and the new blend, and here blend most successfully and happily.

Other Sioux Indians, who live very badly and, unlike the Lower Brule family mentioned, do not seem happy are those on the Lake Traverse Reservation. This reservation is split between northeastern South Dakota and southeastern North Dakota. It has 16,000 residents, but only 2,000 of these are Indians (members of the Sisseton–Wahpeton Band of Sioux Indians) because the land was opened to whites.

Conditions on this reservation are very poor. There is no industry, and the Indians depend upon agriculture, which is not very productive. The average annual income of an Indian family is around $2,000. Since 53 percent of the Indians are under sixteen years of age, the majority cannot contribute to the family income. The tribe as a whole cannot help its members much for it has very little income and very little operating capital. Its holdings are only 850 acres of poor land. However, these Sioux have won a claims settlement in payment for lands they originally owned in Minnesota, Iowa and South Dakota. These funds will be available in the coming years, but today life is not very pleasant. The housing is extremely poor, and there are crowded living conditions. In one case, eight Indian families were living in a former funeral parlor that had only one toilet. Many of the houses on the reservation are still without water, although seventy-one homes were scheduled to get water this past year.

Life for these Indians is a vicious circle. Since there is no industry, very few Indians are employed, except at one local creamery. This lack of income has in turn helped foster the number one health problem on the reservation: alcoholism. According to the secretary of the tribal health council, "practically 100 percent of the population is affected one way or another. . . . The Indians are often driven out of their homes [because of the poor housing conditions] and the only places open for them to hang around are the taverns. Wholesome recreation in a center where there is an adequate staff and equipment is a must." A must also is a community family center for neglected and abandoned children, the victims of alcoholism.

Alcoholism became so acute that the Indians designed a program to attack this problem, and the poor nutrition that goes with it. At this writing they were awaiting a grant from the Department of Health, Education and Welfare for the project.

The tribe has plans for a type of halfway house for alcoholics. There, disturbed and lonely Indians, who are susceptible to drinking, can talk with and counsel one another, and they can get follow-up care after returning from a treatment center. A psychologist will be available, as will be a full-time alcoholism counselor, and a volunteer patrol to pick up intoxicated men on the street and take them home before they are arrested by police. This patrol will also report on neglected children.

Coupled with this problem of acute alcoholism is the problem of poor relations with the whites in Sisseton. The Indians claim that the white stores charge too much for goods, and the whites claim that the Indians are not only drunkards, but shiftless.

What a sorry situation these Indians find themselves in!

The Oglala Sioux's Pine Ridge Reservation in South Dakota has often been cited as an example of wretched living conditions for Indians on the reservations. "From the standpoint of world poverty, the Oglalas would not be considered poor, but in the United States, their living conditions would place them among the nation's most economically depressed minority groups. . . ." a recent study reported. These Oglala Sioux do not personally look like a "poverty-stricken population." There are no obvious signs of undernourishment, and their clothing is neither shabby nor inadequate. The Indians seem neat and well-dressed. However, the signs of poverty are to be found in the physical surroundings—in their housing, which is as miserable as can be. More than half the reservation homes are made of logs caulked with mud and some of the families live permanently in tents. Only about 9 percent of the homes have electricity, 5 percent or less have running water and bathrooms, most of the families transport water more than a quarter of a mile. There is also tremendous overcrowding: 21 percent of the people live in one-room houses, and there is one household of twenty-one persons living in a one-room house.

Researchers have discovered many dangerous signs of social disorganization in the Oglala culture. There is disintegration of the family unit, interfamily strife, drinking, delinquency, child neglect and behavior problems. The rate of suicide attempts among the Indians at Pine Ridge is over five times higher than the estimated national rate. Crime rates are higher too. The arrest rate among Pine Ridge Indians is three times higher than for Indians in general and over sixteen times higher than the national rate. Arrests for drunkenness are twenty-five times higher than the U.S. rates; vandalism, thirty-five times higher; disorderly conduct, twenty times higher. And almost half of the offenses committed by Pine Ridge Indians are directly related to alcohol.

Researchers in this study of the Oglala Sioux concluded that the drinking, like the delinquency, is a "reaction to the frustrations attending lack of meaningful employment and poverty . . . drinking became a socially acceptable means of escaping from unbearable realities. . . ."

These Oglala Indians have plenty of land. The reservation consists of an area of a little less than 3 million acres, and over half of this is owned by the Indians (though in 1942 the War Department took a large piece of it for use as an aerial gunnery range). There are about 11,000 Oglala Indians, yet only a little more than 200 families are successfully engaged in farming. About half the labor force is without jobs. Since the average annual income is a little over $2,000, almost half the reservation's families receive some type of welfare assistance. In about 36 percent of the Indian households *no one* works. Of those who do, many work for some type of government agency on the reservation. There were several fishhook factories on the reservation, but they closed down in 1968. Now there is only a moccasin factory. Some Indians ranch, but over a quarter of the population is dependent on seasonable employment, mostly harvesting potatoes and beets in Nebraska.

What can be done to help these Indians? A million and one industrial, economic, and financial projects could be considered, and many developed, but here there must be a boost given to the Indians themselves, as individuals. Somehow or other those aspects of their culture that have become weakened must become strengthened. These Indians need dignity. They can be helped by eliminating their dependent poverty, through the creation of job opportunities, which could become available through bringing industries to the reservation, starting small businesses, promoting tourism and increasing the Indian land holdings. The educational system could be upgraded; Indian leadership could be encouraged and strengthened. There is much to be done by Indians and non-Indians alike. And it can be done.

That Indian morale can be raised, and raised high, was indicated by the change in atmosphere on the Rosebud Indian Reservation, which adjoins that of the Oglala Sioux. Here on almost 4 million acres live 7,000 Indians, farming, ranching and working as manual laborers in the two industries which are located on the reservation. The tribe has some assets (about $24 million) which it gets from leasing its lands to Indians and non-Indians for ranching and farming.

A few years ago the Indian leaders surveyed their situation. There was enough tribal money to develop a tourist attraction in one of the canyons. Yet half the Indians were unemployed.

Equally important, most of the Indians were living in slums. They lived in car bodies, tents, log huts and shacks, in shanties and even converted windowless chicken coops. The "houses" had dirt floors and were lit by oil lamps. Water often was far away.

The tribal council knew something had to be done, and they turned to the federal government. Funds were secured from the Department of Housing and Urban Development; the Division of Indian Health installed water and sewage systems. The Office of Economic Opportunity and the Bureau of Indian Affairs furnished funds for training programs and equipment—and since that time almost 1,000 new housing units have been constructed, with the help of the Indians, on the reservation. This could have been called "Operation Bootstrap." The change in morale was like the change from night to day.

Now the tribe is going on to push for further projects, to bring industries to the reservation, to provide better and more employment. One Indian leader said the future could be exciting, for he saw what the tribal council had done, and all the possibilities in the coming years. No longer would the tribal council be just a political entity, but would become in reality a management corporation, doing for the Indians much of what in the past has been done by others.

11

THE INDIANS OF
THE CENTRAL STATES

Some of the states in the central portion of America have relatively few Indians. One such state is Nebraska where 2,000 poverty-stricken people live on the reservations. The average income of these Indians is about $1,500 per year, and housing is poor. Unemployment is above the national average for Indians and the high school dropout rate is about double the national average for all students. Again one sees the pattern: need for proper development of the resources, and furthermore, need for qualified and experienced tribal leadership, so that the tribe can successfully develop within limited frameworks.

The Omaha tribe on the eastern edge of the state is an example of how some of the Nebraska Indians live.

The members built their own homes around 1900, and since the homes are relatively old they are in need of repair. No new federal homes have been built.

In 1952 the Bureau of Indian Affairs withdrew, discontinued the high school and turned the grade school over to the state.

The tribe has the largest elementary enrollment in the county, yet has fewer high school graduates than other county schools. Of fifty or more youngsters starting ninth grade, only three will graduate at the end of four years.

Half of the tribe is unemployed. About fifteen members farm, on a small scale, usually part-time, in addition to their regular jobs. Several work in nearby towns, serve in the military, or are employed by the federal or state government. Some work for the Office of Economic Opportunity, the tribe or the Public Health Service. Some own businesses.

Most members belong to the Native American (Indian) Church. Other faiths have left no mark on the membership, so very few attend the white man's religious institutions. "The Omaha believe in God the Father, his son Jesus Christ and the Holy Ghost, long before the white man came to this land," said one tribesman.

Very little culture has been retained—only a powwow in August where the Indians wear authentic costumes and dance and sing. "Things are changing. Although it is sad to some degree—it has to be this way in order to survive in today's world.

"Death comes early to the Omaha—life expectancy is short —and alcohol is the cause for most deaths—accidental death rate is high and suicide is increasing," the tribesman continued. As to the future: "Eventually we'll assimilate in the white culture in order to exist." It is unfortunate that the Omaha do not speak of hope, but grimly speak of the desperate need to assimilate into a white society.

Some of the same despair can be found among the Indians of Oklahoma, but in this state there is a vast variation in the lives of the Indians, perhaps because the Indians of Oklahoma have had an unusual background. Today they number 60,000, a population second only to the Indians of Arizona, and yet these Indians all live differently, some accepting the white man's society, and excelling in it, and others retaining native language and customs.

There are some Indians who have attained prominence in the professions, and some who have reached top administrative positions in major companies. And, conversely, there are the poverty-stricken who need all the assistance available to them.

Oklahoma is really the melting pot of Indians, for in the beginning, in the sixteenth century when the Spanish came across them, there were probably only half a dozen Indian tribes. Today, there are sixty-eight.

Of the many Indian tribes which were moved by the federal government into the area that became Oklahoma, most prominent were the Five Civilized Tribes, so named because of their high degree of cultural development: the Cherokees, Chickasaws, Choctaws, Creeks, and Seminoles. After the Civil War these tribes lost the western part of their area, as punishment by the United States because they had helped the Confederates. The government then began assigning the land to displaced and landless Indians from Kansas and other states. The later establishment of trading posts, the rights-of-way for public highways, cattle drives, the railroad rights—all cut into the land, as did opening the area to white homesteading. Finally the Allotment Act of 1887 broke up the Indian reservations, as Indian lands passed from tribal ownership to individual Indian owners. There are no reservations today, and of the original 30 million acres allotted to the Indians, little more than 1.6 million acres remain in Indian hands.

Today the majority of these Indians live among the general

population; the exceptions are some communities in which full-blooded Indians predominate, mostly in rural sections. Many of these live in poverty, while other Indians, with oil and gas discovered on their lands, receive handsome incomes.

One of the Indian tribes in Oklahoma which has successfully moved into the mainstream of the state is the Wyandotte tribe, which has 1,150 members on its roll, and owns, as a tribe, only a two-and-one-half-acre cemetery in the middle of Kansas City, Kansas.

These Indians, without land, still live as a tribe, with a governing committee, whose members are elected every two years by a majority vote of the membership present. The tribe, as such, does not operate any industries, but some of the tribesmen own their own farms that operate on a large scale. They own modern machinery, tractors, combines, and so on. Only a very small percentage of working age are unemployed, and the average annual income is about $6,000—a fabulous sum when compared to the average $1,500 Indian income in the nation.

These Indians really do not have "Indian" situations or "Indian" problems. As one of them said, they have adopted the white man's ways and as a whole have a good life. They have good housing, good schools, good health, and health facilities. Crafts and tribal culture have long been forgotten and the Indians are "citizens of this country."

Perhaps the only "Indian" problem one could speak of is the settlement of claims which are now pending before the Claims Commission. These Wyandottes have a staff of lawyers on a percentage basis, taking care of this matter, and they are waiting for the results.

Another group of Indians located in the eastern section of Oklahoma are those of the vast tribe of the Cherokee Nation.

It is perhaps illuminating to read what the Cherokees themselves report on their lives today.

It is estimated that there are between 80,000 and 100,-000 persons of some degree of Cherokee Indian blood ranging from a full blood degree to a 1/256 degree, as evidenced by approved final roll of the Cherokee tribe of Oklahoma. These individuals live throughout Oklahoma, the nation and in some foreign countries.

Cherokee Indians are full citizens of the State, many took their places as outstanding leaders of Oklahoma, in the Congress of the United States, serving on the courts of Oklahoma and in both houses of the State Legislature, and they have continued to add immeasurably to the cultural and spiritual life, to the wealth and stability of Oklahoma. When the Cherokee arrived in what is now Oklahoma, they had already gone far in the fields of Christianity, education, complex tribal organization and tribal government.

Today the principal chief of the Cherokee Nation of Oklahoma is the Honorable W. W. Keeler, who is chairman of the board of the Phillips Petroleum Company. Along with an executive committee, elected community representatives, and heads of organized Cherokee groups, he governs the tribe.

The Cherokees are employed in the same professions and fields of endeavor as other citizens. However, this is not to say that all Cherokees have reached this level in life. There is a certain segment of the Cherokee Indian population, living in remote, rural communities, who, because of lack of education, business experience, and the language barrier, live at a rather low level of existence.

The Cherokee occupies the same type of housing, some very good and some bad, as his non-Indian neighbor, interspersed throughout the communities. Considerable improvement is being made at this time in housing and improved sanitation facilities for the Cherokee families through federal and tribal programs.

Education based upon Christian principles and teachings was the goal for which the Cherokees have always worked.

A most interesting fact, since generally one does not associate Indians with the establishment of free public education in this country, is the following:

A public school system was established in 1841 by the Cherokees which was supported by appropriations of the Cherokee National Council from education funds. There were eighteen public schools in operation in 1843, the number continued to increase to more than 120 during the last days of the Cherokee tribal government a half century later. The first institutions of free public education were the Cherokee Male and Female seminaries established in Tahlequah, capital of the Cherokee Nation, in 1851. These schools were the forerunners of the present Northeastern State College today located at Tahlequah.

Since Oklahoma statehood (which was accomplished with the Cherokees and other of the Five Civilized tribes playing an important part), the Cherokee students have been enrolled in public schools. There have been in addition, federally maintained Indian boarding schools for special classes of Indian students.

Strides are being made in establishing industry within the Cherokee area through tribal programming; the Bureau of Indian Affairs and private industry in the State of Oklahoma. Indians are receiving on-the-job training and progress is being made. . . . Farming is practiced by some of the tribal members with excellent results. However, not all Cherokees prefer to do farming, some are poor farmers. . . . The Cherokees operate a Cherokee Arts–Crafts Center at the Cherokee Tribal Complex and a subdivision near Catoosa, Oklahoma, on the Will Rogers Turnpike. These are new enterprises and they are growing. . . .

Incomes range from very low income to salaries comparable to many non-Indians of the area. However, those in the low income brackets are very definitely in the majority.

The biggest problem [of the tribe] is economic. Every effort is being made . . . to improve the social and economic conditions of the Cherokees.

Thus it can be seen, in Oklahoma, as elsewhere that there are vast ranges in conditions of the Indians in America. Some have succeeded very well in the white man's world, some have not. Some want to be of that world, others do not.

The Indians of Texas are very unlike the Oklahoma Indians who are greatly absorbed into the white culture. About 360 members of the Alabama and Choushatta tribes live on Texas' only Indian reservation, and have retained their own culture to a great degree. The native language is spoken in the home, and often the first exposure to English is when a child attends school.

These tribes still excel in crafts. They are experts in pine-straw basket making, weaving, silver work, and pottery, and their wares are sold at the trading post which is operated by the tribal enterprise.

This reservation has a slightly different relationship with the government. In 1954, the federal government gave up its trusteeship of the land, and the reservation is now under the jurisdiction of the tribe and a special state agency for Indian affairs. Thus the federal benefits given to many other Indian reservations are not available here. Because of the limited comprehension of the English language, and the lack of job opportunities, many of these Indians find it difficult to get work. To remedy this situation, the tribe has set up an enterprise to promote tourist attractions on the reservation, which employs tribal members as cooks, waitresses, dancers, sales clerks, secretaries and drivers.

For the tourists there is a museum, arts and crafts shop, and a restaurant which offers Indian food, such as sofkey, a corn dish, fry bread, and bar-b-que dishes. An authentic dance square, patterned on the earlier dance squares used by the tribes hundreds of years ago, is the site of tribal dances by the *Na-Ski-La* Dancers. There is the living Indian village where tribal members cook food, make pottery, beadwork, basketry, arrowheads, weapons, leather and woodcraft, in a village setting of 1805. There is a nature trail where over eighty shrubs, trees, and flowers are identified. There is a Big Thicket Tour, which goes through the pine trees (much of the land is pine-covered forest) and swamp.

The tribes are planning more for the future—the construction of a 600-acre lake, canoe trips, camping areas, covered wagon rides, boat docks, and fishing areas. By taking advantage of their culture, and the beauty of the area, these tribes are sustaining themselves by showing the public Texas' only Indian reservation.

For many years the Alabama–Coushatta tribes were considered by the general public to be the only Indian groups in Texas. However, citizens of El Paso knew about the Tigua Indians. These were a displaced Pueblo tribe which originally lived south of Albuquerque, New Mexico. During the Pueblo revolt of 1680 the tribe was removed by the Spanish and located at Ysleta, El Paso, where they built the present Ysleta Mission. It was not until 1967 that they came to public attention, when their homes were threatened by tax foreclosure proceedings. Then they were formally recognized as a Texas tribe, and placed in trust capacity. In 1968 they were given federal recognition.

These Ysleta Tigua Indians still practice many customs no longer found among other Pueblo people. They still have the basic aboriginal form of tribal government which was in use when the Spanish found them; they still do the ancient ceremonial dances and continue to live in the same kind of houses and get much of their food by hunting, fishing, and the planting of small gardens. They still use herbs, roots and plants for medicine. Now that they have come to public attention, they will receive help in operating tourist attractions.

One certainly cannot stress too much the extreme variance in the conditions and positions of the Indians, so well illustrated by these Indians who live in the central part of the country. On the one hand a Cherokee is in a leadership position in the nation, and on the other hand there are Indians who still hunt and fish and live as Indians did many years ago. The future seems, too, to be as diverse as the Indians who wait for it.

12

THE INDIANS
OF THE GREAT LAKES

The Indians in the Great Lakes area are scattered, and do not generally live in large groups as do those of the western states. There are large cultural and economic gaps between those Indians who live on remote reservations and the general society around them. Those who live on rural reservations have maintained many of their tribal traditions. At the other extreme in the cultural pattern are the Indians who have moved to nearby cities, such as Green Bay, Chicago, or Milwaukee. They have found jobs, their children go to the public schools, and generally they have a higher standard of living than those in remote areas.

One of the problems facing the Indians in some of these areas is not strictly an Indian problem, it is the problem of the very land on which they live. For example, The Mole Lake Band of the Sokaogan Chippewa community in Wisconsin lives on land that has unproductive swamps and low-grade timber. The area is definitely depressed, and the 115 Indians here pick rice late in summer, and trap muskrat and mink. They also gather ferns, boughs and pine cones for a limited income. They seem very isolated from members of the general community around them. The Potawatomis in the Forest County Potawatomi community also live in one of the depressed areas in Wisconsin, and here too, these 230 Indians are isolated from non-Indian activities outside the reservation. Many of them are full-blooded, and often speak in their native language. They are basically dependent upon welfare grants by the county welfare department.

The Wisconsin Winnebago tribe has a larger population, over a thousand members, but they occupy scattered settlements, and the rural areas in which they live are among the poorest of Wisconsin; thus the standard of living of this tribe is very low. Most of these Indians have become migratory, depending on seasonal employment such as work on the roads, forestry projects, construction work, and tourist entertainment. Oddly enough, these Indians are considered to have done more than any other Indians in Wisconsin in promoting Indian culture through their excellent handcrafts, which supply a limited income.

The conditions under which the Indians of the rural areas live is disheartening. As the Wisconsin Governor's Commission on Human Rights pointed out, many of the reservations are not wilderness paradises; many could be described as "forest poorhouses where the inhabitants live . . . on the bitter edge of poverty." They have poor housing and poor health and they depend upon welfare. However, the commission discovered, this situation was not a result of the residents being Indian, as is often the case, but rather as a result of living in areas of northern Wisconsin in which there are few opportunities for steady, year-round employment.

The commission found that there was something happening in these areas, and that was a "freshening wind of leadership from among the Indians themselves." Indians are speaking out and trying to take action. This has resulted in a "broad interest in discovering these forgotten citizens and in acknowledging responsibility toward them." This new interest has not as yet had any positive result, for the commission found that the economic position of the Indians had not improved significantly over the past fifteen years and that the communities still have a "gray look of desolation," but that the psychological climate among the Indians has indeed changed from hopelessness to optimism.

Not all of the Great Lakes Indians endure such poverty conditions. Those who live in, or near, white communities have fared much better. Take, for example, the members of the Red Cliff Chippewa Band who live on a reservation located along Lake Superior. They have intermarried with non-Indians, and they participate with adjoining communities in social activities as well as local government. Obviously they have not retained any of their Indian language or customs. They find work in the nearby industries, or seasonal work on the orchards and berry farms, in resorts, and with the fisheries during the herring runs.

The Lac Courte Oreilles Chippewa Band of Indians is also fortunate that its 750 members on the reservation can find employment. A factory was established, and it has proved very successful, and a cranberry marsh was developed with a federal government loan of $135,000. This provides employment in harvesting and packing the crop and tending the marshes. In addition, instead of being in a remote rural area, the reservation is in a top tourist area of Wisconsin, so seasonal work is available at the resorts, hotels, and motels. Also there are jobs all year around in the forest products industry. All this—and yet the individual Indian income is today only $1,500 per year.

Obviously, these Indians need help, definite concrete aid that will give them more jobs and more money, and a more dignified way of life. But, as the commission pointed out, the solution does not lie in "help from above in the form of handouts or programs which someone else thinks will be good for him." These can accomplish little.

> Today the Indian, more than a little weary and suspicious of outside efforts to improve his condition, desperately needs understanding; and any aid he receives should be based on an intelligent recognition of his determination to maintain his Indian identity. . . . Progress will come with cooperative endeavor that allows the Indian to exercise his own qualities of leadership in planning and deciding and determining his destiny.

The more the leaders of these Indians can and will speak out, the more they plan for their own futures, the more effective aid to them can be. Their problems are at long last recognized by many. Now is the time to help the Indians help themselves.

13

THE INDIANS OF THE EASTERN SEABOARD

The vast expanse of land to the east and south of the Great Lakes region, all the way to the eastern seaboard, has little organized Indian population. There are, however, large numbers of Indians in the urban centers here as elsewhere in the country, but it is only on the eastern seaboard that there are any significant number living on reserved lands.

In New England there are, perhaps, 6,000 Indians, living on non-federal reservations from Maine to Connecticut. In Maine, these reservations have never been under federal jurisdiction, like those in the western part of the country, but are supervised by the state. The Indians live in small communities and work in nearby mills, in the shipyards, in business firms, and in logging.

Only a very few Indians still live in New Hampshire and Vermont, and these are without either state or federal supervision. In Massachusetts there are a number of scattered Indian settlements, with perhaps a total of 2,000 Indians. One of the tribes, the Wampanoags, owns its own town at Gay Head in Martha's Vineyard. Here 200 Indians still make pottery and beadwork. Connecticut has perhaps eighteen Indians, although there are still four reservations (mainly uninhabited), held in trusteeship by the state.

Of the northeastern states only New York State has a significant Indian population, and in recent years Indians here have been speaking out about the need to organize, so that they could become a power to be reckoned with. About 10,000 Indians live on about 80,000 acres of reservation land. Most prominent are the Six Nations of the Iroquois League—the Mohawks, Oneidas, Onondagas, Cayugas, Senecas and Tuscaroras (originally from North Carolina, who have been taken in as the sixth nation).

Of all these Indians, the Senecas, with three separate reservations, have the largest enrolled membership, almost 5,000 individuals. They own the city of Salamanca, which they have leased to the city, and for which they receive rental each year.

Among the New York Indians, one finds the same long-time pattern of usurpation of lands. Recently some of the land of the Tuscarora Reservation, which is near Niagara Falls, was taken by the state for a reservoir. The Indians were paid $850,000 for the land loss, but it is a shame to see in such cases that the government has not really changed its policies.

To New York State's credit, however, it must be mentioned that since the Indian lands have been under its jurisdiction, the Indians are provided with services, which are otherwise provided by tax-supported local governments. Matters relating to health, education, and welfare are all handled by the state, as are highways, conservation, employment assistance, and many other services. The aim today in New York State is to help the

Indians help themselves, to make sure that they make use of the many kinds of assistance that are available to all citizens. Only thus, so state officials feel, can the Indians take their "rightful place in the community and make their cultural contributions to the community."

As for the rest of the East, there are a few Indians today in Delaware, Maryland, Pennsylvania and Virginia. It is interesting—if depressing again—to note that the Cornplanter Reservation given to the Indians in Pennsylvania is now unoccupied because of the construction of the Kinzua Dam. Some of the tribal members in Virginia still live by hunting and fishing, and also make some pottery and beadwork which they sell to the tourists, while others, like the Chickahominy, who are the largest group in Virginia, pay taxes, own their own land and send their children to public schools.

The largest Indian reservation in the eastern United States is farther south, in western North Carolina. Here almost 5,000 members of the Eastern Band of Cherokee Indians live on a reservation which is still under federal trusteeship.

The Cherokee Reservation in the heart of the Smoky Mountains has often been called a model reservation, for the tribal members are active and industrious and have established a fairly sound economic base.

In earlier days, the Cherokees had a very difficult time in America. In the 1830's, as a result of a treaty with the federal government, the Cherokees were to move west of the Mississippi. What took place then has been called "The Trail of Tears." About 14,000 Cherokees began an 800-mile journey on foot, in winter, to the Indian territory which now forms Oklahoma. At this time about 1,000 Cherokees refused to go and hid in the mountains. These were to be the Eastern Band of the

Cherokees, and they were, after much hardship, formally granted title to a reservation almost forty years later.

This land is forested and mountainous, so farming is limited, but many Cherokees work in the forests. Timber is sold each year by the tribe to individual members who then market saw-logs and other forest products. There is a good community spirit. Community buildings have been constructed; there are seven civic clubs. The tribe owns and operates its own fleet of school buses, and it has an auto mechanic shop. A farm club for young people provides practical leadership training. There are three industrial plants on the reservation, and a commercial tourism industry has been developed. Housing has been built. Plans have been made for the construction of a new high school for which the Eastern Band has already appropriated $80,000 for the purchase of the land.

The main portion of the reservation is at the major entry to Great Smoky Mountain Park, so the tourist activity is high. The Band owns and operates a motel, lodge, dining room, snack bar and service station. It has a tribal cooperative and market-ing center for Cherokee Indian crafts. The baskets, wood carv-ings, beadwork, handwoven linen and woolen fabrics are out-standing, and provide a good income.

The Cherokees themselves see their needs as better education and job training, improved economic opportunities, better roads, better housing, and the development of better overall plans for their future.

Their situation is so superior to that of many Indian tribes, it is no wonder that they have been called a model reservation. Yet here, too, there are the problems of entering more and more into the American mainstream. One non-Indian official feels that the biggest problem for the Cherokee Indians will be to

Hayes Lossie demonstrates the ancient Cherokee art of dart making at Oconaluftee Indian Village, North Carolina

maintain the strength of the family and the tribal government in a time when there are many forces brought by change and growth straining against these social institutions. Coupled with this is the need to improve the education—to have the families, and the community as a whole, place higher value on educational achievement, and then to have the federal government supply enough funds to improve educational facilities.

If the family and the tribal government remain stable, then the individual has a greater chance for personal success, as this non-Indian observer stated, an opportunity "to be born, to grow and to develop in an area where he has a feeling of worth and dignity."

As for the tribe as a whole, the non-Indian commented:

The Cherokees have many economic assets including beautiful land located in an important tourist center, a good proximity to the best markets in this country, and a group of people who can well hold their heads high in terms of past accomplishments in spite of many adverse circumstances, including the taking over of their lands by this country, their tragic removal to Oklahoma, and their location in what has in the past been an economically depressed area. The future of the Eastern Band of Cherokee Indians should be bright if the people will establish sound goals and work cooperatively toward meeting them, and if the general public can continue to maintain empathy and support for programs of assistance needed by the Cherokees to carry out such goals.

The story of the Catawbas in South Carolina is a sad one. In the eighteenth century, they were granted a reservation fifteen miles square. By 1841 all of the land was sold but one square

mile. Then in 1943 the state gave them monies for land and
other purposes, and the Catawbas were declared citizens of the
state of South Carolina. There was federal aid, and the land was
divided among individuals for homesites and gardens, and one
portion was kept for timber and cattle range. By 1954 it was
said that the Catawbas had progressed more in the preceding
decade than any other tribe in the United States. This was the
time that termination was in the air, and it came to the Catawbas. By 1961 their ties to the federal government were severed
and the Indians no longer received special Indian services.
Tribal lands and monies were divided among the members.
There is no longer a reservation, and no longer a flourishing
tribal culture. A few of the older women make pottery, but that
is all.

Here again a thoughtless, shortsighted government destroyed
the base of success for an Indian tribe. Like the Klamaths, in
Oregon, one wonders where they would be today if the thinking
about termination had been then, as it is now.

14

THE INDIANS OF FLORIDA

Early in the eighteenth century when the Indians came drifting down into Florida, the Seminoles received their name—*Is-te Seminole* for "Wild People"—to set them apart from the "tame Indians who had stayed near the whites." It is an apt description for the Seminole wars are famous.

The first war came in 1818 when General Andrew Jackson marched into Florida and defeated the Indians. Jackson then occupied Spanish cities, killed Indians, and seized Negro slaves, until finally Spain, unable to defend Florida, was forced to turn the territory over to the United States. Then followed years of wars, when many of the Seminoles were forced to relocate in Oklahoma Territory. At long last when the government troops were withdrawn from Florida, there were only about 150 Seminoles left. They were scattered throughout southern Florida, having broken up into family groups or clans. They lived a nomadic life, existing mostly by hunting and fishing from thatched-roof chickees, built of cypress poles and palmetto leaves which protected them from the rains and the hot sun. The same type of chickees are still in use on two of the three reservations of the Seminoles where today 1,060 Indians live.

The Hollywood Reservation has only 475 acres, but it is very valuable land, since the city of Hollywood has grown up around it. There is tremendous potential for industrial development: high-rise apartments, shopping plazas, etc. Here the tribe has forbidden its members to live in the chickees, and there are modern homes. Because there is so much activity in this area, many of the Indians have come from the other two, more isolated, reservations, seeking employment, so that there is now a population of about 350 on the reservation.

There has been phenomenal development by the Indians in the past quarter of a century. The tribe did not formally organize until 1957; then for the first time they had a group of leaders who could work with the government to raise the standard of living for their people. The Indians had for many years lived in wilderness and swamplands, avoiding contacts with the whites, preserving their ancient way of life. It took, as one tribal member said recently:

> almost a 100 years for them to forget the war and their hatred and distrust of all but a very few whites. However, in the last few years the wall between the two races has crumbled; their children are in white schools; the Seminoles are coming more and more into the ways of their white neighbors; and the hands of the two ancient enemies are clasped in friendship.

Today, in addition to the Hollywood Reservation, there is the Brighton Reservation with 35,796 acres, and the Big Cypress Reservation of 42,697 acres developed in the 1930's. At Brighton the majority of the people speak a Crow–Creek dialect. Their homes have been substandard for many years, but with the help of the Bureau of Indian Affairs and others, new homes are going up, to join the chickees. On this reservation some of the Indians are cattlemen, others work as cowboys on ranches, or in the fields as farm hands. Some make handcrafts for souvenirs, and the Seminole tribe has a textile shop, a trading post, and a cattle-raising enterprise.

On Big Cypress most of the people speak the Miccosukee tongue (of a different Florida tribe) and have a different culture from those on the other two reservations. They also earn their living as cattlemen and farm hands. There is a trading post, and most of the Indians are first-class woodcarvers, using the native cypress wood, to make more souvenirs than the other two reservations put together. The majority of the people live in chickees. Most recently though, some money has been available to families for home improvement, which means modified chickees.

As a whole the Seminoles are employed off and on the reservations. In addition to the occupations cited above, some are orange-grove workers, heavy-equipment operators, welders, carpenters, barbers, construction workers on buildings and roads, thatched-roof hut contractors, and alligator wrestlers. There is some industry on the land—a white-owned electronic parts manufacturer leases land from the tribe, and there will be a factory to build homes. Money has been sought to develop an area on Brighton Reservation for an industrial complex.

A tribal official reports that farming is not practiced directly by the tribe. However, acreage at Brighton and Big Cypress is leased to large farmers who clear land, ditch and dike, plant three or four crops of vegetables per year and harvest them. In these operations quite a few Seminoles are hired. When farm leases are terminated the land is leveled and seeded to grass, making it improved pastureland for tribal and individual cattle operations. The cattlemen are given guidance by the agricultural school of the University of Florida and by experts under BIA. The Seminoles are known for their fine strain of cattle and have been ranchers for many years.

Some Seminoles work part-time, January through March, under white contractors, cutting palm spikes from trees on Brighton Reservation to be used in churches on Palm Sunday. It is planned some time in the future that this business will be operated completely by the Seminoles themselves.

The average annual income is under $3,000. But here, too, financial and economic conditions vary greatly. There are many elderly Indians on the reservations who are left helpless in the wintertime and do not have enough food for their families.

The lack of education has been a handicap to the Seminoles. Not too many years ago the Indians were not allowed to go to public schools in the State of Florida, so the Seminole students went to North Carolina. Now all the eligible Seminole students are going to public schools in Florida, or to boarding schools in Oklahoma, and for higher education to colleges and to a commercial school in Haskell, Kansas. When these youths return to the reservations, the communities will be much stronger because the young people will have been exposed to twentieth-century modernization. According to a tribal official, much of the culture of the tribe has been retained, but mostly through the middle-aged and the old.

A tourist attraction, the Seminole Okalee Indian Village, is operated on the Hollywood Reservation on U.S. 41 and here a great effort is made to retain and show to the public the methods of making crafts, sewing, beadwork, basketwork, carving small items of all types, and making dugout canoes. The Seminoles are experts in these crafts.

There are chickees on the grounds, where corn-grinding and cooking over an open fire are demonstrated. Everyone working in the village wears traditional and contemporary Seminole clothing, as do many of the Seminoles all the time.

An effort is being made to put up a museum in the not too distant future and some progress has been made in this direction. Powwows are held each year, not just for amusement, but "to promote the Seminole tribe of Florida and also to try to raise enough money for a Seminole Indian museum." What they are trying to accomplish is to bring Indian heritage, which has been handed down from generation to generation, to the public and let them know about the American Indian's way of life. "Television and movies have branded us as savages," said one Indian, "it has not been good for the American Indian. . . . We hope, through the powwow, that you may understand a little more about the 'unconquered Seminole.' "

Tribal officials feel that the biggest problem facing the tribe is the lack of education on the part of those who are over thirty-five, and the language barrier. Adult classes of various kinds have been formed but they are not attended by the older people; the younger people, who have only a few years of schooling, desire more education and do attend.

Through careful and astute handling of its affairs concerning the land, the tribe can become almost entirely self-sufficient. With higher education for the young, the leaders of the tribe hope eventually to have Seminoles in various professions which will benefit all. The young are very aggressive, and for the most part they do not choose to "just wait and see," as has been done previously. They want to "make" the future of the tribe.

The Seminoles recently were awarded over $12 million for land taken away from them by United States military forces. This was a settlement long overdue, for the suit had been filed twenty years before, after Congress established the Claims Commission. One tribal member said: ". . . my people are patiently awaiting betterment of their reservation life. I know someday soon the Seminole Indians, as well as other American Indian tribes, will live comfortably." There does seem hope now.

In 1961, some of the Indians who spoke a different language from the Seminoles and lived along the Tamiami Trail formed the Miccosukee tribe of Indians of Florida. Today this tribe has 230 enrolled members and 220 not enrolled. They live along the Tamiami Trail (U.S. 41) between Miami and Naples, Florida, with the greatest concentration living near Forty-Mile Bend on a strip of land five-and one-half miles by 500 feet, secured by permit between the National Park Service and the Bureau of Indian Affairs. They also have a state trust reservation of 78,600 acres which is undeveloped and on which no one lives.

The Miccosukee tribe has been recognized as a tribe only since 1962, but since that time through the help of the Bureau of Indian Affairs, who provided a loan, the tribe has developed an enterprise of a restaurant, service station, and grocery store on the Tamiami Trail. Here too is an old Indian village, with a community kitchen, chickees, and gardens in which potatoes and other vegetables grow.

The BIA has constructed a modern, two-classroom school and community facilities, and operates an educational program.

Miccosukee Restaurant on the Tamiami Trail, Florida

However, according to the BIA, a "lack of academic background and job skills . . . bring about less than average economic well-being."

The biggest problem today is education. The means for education are available, but the Indians must be encouraged to accept such means. One worker said, "The Miccosukee will in time be as progressive as any other Indian group, and it will have been accomplished through education." A community action worker with the Miccosukee tribe wrote: "This proud, intelligent, beautiful people expect and plan to survive."

15

THE URBAN INDIANS

One cannot speak of the American Indians today without speaking of the urban Indians—the Indians who have left the reservations for the cities to find employment and a better way of life, for there are hundreds of thousands of them in this country today, and as each tribe is different from the others, and each tribal member different from one another, so each urban Indian is an individual, with individual problems. Some of these Indians have adjusted well, and prosper. Some have become broken, poverty-stricken, and ill. As one of the participants at hearings on the urban Indians stated in San Francisco in 1969, "Because of not being properly orientated to urban living, Indians directly from the reservation often find it very hard to adjust to the city way of life."

Frustration and depression usually set in when they find out that people and things are not as they were on the reservation, and they are unable to find jobs because of lack of education and training. (Many have not finished high school.) After about a month or two of trying to find work in the city, many turn to drinking. This type of escape from reality only leads them deeper into despair. Alcoholism among urban Indians is intense.

Many agencies try to help the Indians in the cities, with job assistance, training, education, housing, and health, but many of the Indians are not aware of the facilities available to them, or they seek some type of help and are rebuffed because the particular agency does not have jurisdiction, or adequate staff and money. Many Indians in urban areas are bitter about the Bureau of Indian Affairs, the discrimination they endure, and the type of justice that is meted out to them. (In one case, an Indian boy was given a very stiff prison sentence for possession of a few marijuana cigarettes, while, at the same time, a professional pusher received a lesser sentence for possession of a large quantity of drugs.)

The feeling has been expressed by many Indians that they are the most "studied" group in the United States, and yet their problems are not treated. Too often, Indian students in urban areas need counselors—Indian counselors—and there is a lack of these. The suicide rate for young Indians is skyrocketing.

The urban Indian child has his difficulties, too, forgetting about the reservation, losing his culture, his sense of identity, and becoming an "asphalt Indian." Then there is the problem facing the elderly in urban areas. As one Indian said, "On my reservation, our people have always concerned themselves with old people, because our old people are who we learn our culture from, who we learn the ways of Indian life, and we're no longer using them for that. We have many old people in the area who are almost totally ignored. They're not useful as far as the Indians are concerned. . . . The old people can teach our young people about being Indian. . . ." Often the older Indian has to go on general assistance. He can live, but not live well.

The problems facing the urban Indians are tremendous because there are so many of them. For example, in San Francisco, there are over 10,000 Indians; in Oakland, 10,000; and in the Los Angeles area 45,000. There are Indians in all the large cities: in New York and Brooklyn, Chicago, Cleveland, Dallas, Denver, St. Paul, Minneapolis, Phoenix.

Obviously many of these Indians need help, and they should have it as other citizens of the country have help. Those who leave the reservation for the city face different problems and needs than those who stay behind. "Living in an environment foreign to him, where he barely knows his next-door neighbor, he seeks to hang on to his Indian identity while attempting to adjust to a different and often frightening way of life."

Many of the cities now have centers and clubs to help the Indians with urban adjustment, such as the center in Chicago which has a family service program, maintains a day camp and tutoring facilities. The Call of the Council Drums in Denver, Colorado, has an Indian staff of counselors who work with newly-arrived families and individuals to find jobs, arrange welfare assistance, or locate adequate housing. In Los Angeles the center helps with job placement and training, recruitment for higher education, recreation, and social welfare. There are centers in New York City, Cleveland, Phoenix, Seattle and Tulsa. Washington, D.C., has the American Indian Society whose goals are:

> to preserve Indian culture and perpetuate Indian tradition; to promote fellowship among members of all American Indian tribes; to enlighten the public and encourage

better understanding of the Indian people and to assist young Indian boys and girls in their academic studies by establishing a scholarship fund.

The Society hopes to improve communication and unity among local Indians on an informal, people-to-people level. A special interest is to encourage young people to join with other Indian people, thereby finding friends with similar background and interests. Newcomers, especially those who may be living in the city for the first time, may have difficulty in adjusting to the crowded, faster-paced urban life. Association with a group of like-minded people helps to make the transition easier. The drums, the dances, the food—all are part of the common Indian heritage.

In 1969 a new organization was formed, called American Indians-United, which represents sixty-two Indian urban centers and groups in cities throughout the nation, and hopes to become a national unified voice for all off-reservation Indians. The AI-U has set itself many tasks: one is to strengthen the urban Indian's identity, "so that he will look upon his heritage as a source of strength and identity rather than a source of weakness and confusion"; another is to obtain for the urban Indian, both from private and federal sources, the same services that are now provided for the reservation Indian, such as housing and education. As its executive director said, "the needs are as great for the Indian in the city as they are for the Indian on the reservation—perhaps even greater, because he is away from friends and family in what amounts to a foreign world."

Dramatic news concerning the urban Indians came in the first month of 1972, when the government announced that it was ending the relocation of Indians. In the past twenty years, over 100,000 Indians had been shipped to the cities, with the help of the BIA, in the hope that they would not only find jobs, but would be assimilated into white urban society.

According to BIA Commissioner Louis R. Bruce, the relocation program had only helped to create "Indian ghettos" in the cities, and fully 40 percent of the Indians went back to their reservations. Now the government's $40 million a year training and job assistance programs will be used to help the Indians *on* the reservations.

As a government spokesman said, "Now, instead of taking ... [the Indians] off and melting them down with their Indian culture, the idea is to give them opportunities on their reservations."

16

THE FUTURE

Perhaps—and only an optimist might go so far—a new day is dawning for the American Indians.

They have been mistreated, neglected, scorned, and "studied" for years, by various segments of the American majority. Individual Indians and even whites have cried out about injustices that the Indians have suffered at the hands of the federal government and about overall poor conditions.

Fifty thousand Indian families live in unsanitary, dilapidated dwellings, many in huts, shanties, or even abandoned automobiles.

The average Indian income is $1,500—75 percent below the national average.

The unemployment rate among Indians is nearly 40 percent —more than ten times the national average.

The average age of death of the American Indian is forty-four years, for all other Americans it is sixty-five.

The infant mortality rate is twice the national average.

Dropout rates are twice the national average in both public and federal schools.

Achievement levels of Indian children are two- to three-years below those of white students.

Only 1 percent of Indian children in elementary schools have Indian teachers or principals.

In the summer of 1970, President Richard Nixon addressed a message to Congress on the Indians, calling them the "most deprived and most isolated minority group in our nation." He spoke of "the heritage of centuries of injustice." He said that even "the federal programs which are intended to meet their needs have frequently proven to be ineffective and demeaning. . . . The time has come to break decisively with the past and create the conditions for a new era in which the Indian future is determined by Indian acts and decisions." The President spoke out against the old policy of termination, the fear of which produced:

> the opposite extreme: excessive dependence on the federal government. In many cases this dependence is so great that the Indian community is almost entirely run by outsiders who are responsible and responsive to federal officials in Washington, D.C., rather than to the communities they are supposed to be serving. The result is a burgeoning federal bureaucracy, programs which are far less effective than they ought to be, and an erosion of Indian initiative and morale.

President Nixon said what many of the Indian leaders have been saying for years. He proposed that Congress pass legislation which would let the Indians run the programs for themselves. This was not a revolutionary or new thought; the Indians have been agitating for years to have control over their own destiny. Included in the President's plan was the right of the Indians to run their own schools. He also proposed the Indian Financing Act of 1970 which would raise by millions the funds available for economic development projects, for health programs, and expanded urban centers.

These were all noble aims and plans and they largely remained just that until January, 1972, when the BIA announced a new five-point program for the Indians. This new federal program was a "redirection of policy," designed to actually give the Indians more control of their own affairs. One point was the discontinuance of the relocation of the Indians to the cities; another was a plan to speed up development programs on the reservations; another, to double the existing $30 million allocated annually for road construction on the reservations; and —at last—more tribal control of Indian education programs. The fifth program involved a new Indian Water Rights Office, with funds of $500,000 to protect the land and water rights of the Indians from encroachment by federal and private interests. And how needed this office is!

The story of the decline of the Paiutes' Pyramid Lake had been publicly known for years. But, early in 1972, Senator Ted Kennedy discovered many more such outrages to Indian water and land. "Western U.S. Indian Reservations Turned Into Scorched Earth" was the headline for a newspaper article detailing Senator Kennedy's investigation and findings. Tribe after tribe poured out their rage at what had happened to their waters. The Trinity River on the Hoopla Valley Reservation in northern California has diminished as upstream dams divert the water; the water table of the Papagoes in southern Arizona has been lowered nearly 200 feet by the pumping of ground water by non-Indians near Indian wells. Over and over, the theme was repeated by dozens of Indian communities.

The Water Rights Office is a step in the right direction. By its surveys it will establish the water rights of the tribes—which hopefully can then be protected. Too often the rights of the Indians are ignored while more powerful groups—government and private—impose their wills. The tribal chairman of the La Jolla Reservation recalled all the futile protests against the power lines put up across their land. Today the tribe still has neither electricity nor any compensation for the use of its lands.

The injustices to the Indians are still many, but now for the first time in many years the federal government policy truly seems to be toward self-determination for the Indians and financial help to assist them in their goals.

Could this be the new day dawning?

Perhaps a new regard for the Indians has become apparent in the white society, and many Indians are determined that they will be heard and that their rights will be respected.

As the decade of the 1970's began, the Indians *were* being heard. There are militant Indians who act and want their actions noted, to call attention to their rights: witness the Indians on Alcatraz. One tribe after another has spoken out for its rights. An angry group of Oglala Sioux maintained a vigil of prayer and fasting on the top of Sheep Mountain in the Badlands, in an effort to have the land taken from them during World War II for an Air Force gunnery range returned.

"We have laid down the tomahawk," said one of the Indians on Sheep Mountain. "We know that a lot of right-thinking Americans are for the underdog. So we continue to put our faith in orderly protest, due process. . . ." The Vice-President of the tribal council said: "The government's still doing the same old thing—taking land away from us and not recognizing us as human beings."

That statement could be balanced by the recent restoration to the Taos Pueblo Indians of New Mexico of their small, sacred Blue Lake and all its 48,000 acre watershed. The Pueblos wanted their land, and with presidential backing, they got it back.

The Three Affiliated Tribes of the Fort Berthold Reservation in North Dakota also want their land back, and if they get it this time it will be the whites who are moved. Do 363,520 acres of land lost to the Indians in 1910 still belong to the Indians or not? The question is up before the courts. One Indian member, displaying wry humor in discussing the Indians' plight here, spoke to a white: "Where we made our big mistake," he said, "was when we let you guys off the Mayflower."

The Navajos have been fighting to prove title to 40 million acres of western land on which they claimed they had roamed for centuries. The Indians Claims Commission recently agreed that the Indians should have been paid for much of that land in 1868 when they were placed on the reservation. A settlement will be the result.

The Six Iroquois Tribes of New York met some months ago to explore the possibility of forming a statewide organization that would give the tribes political power in Washington and Albany. What a modern viewpoint, compared to the past when the traditionalists, grouped around the hereditary chiefs, sought to maintain the integrity of each reservation and of the old culture. The more progressive Indians are now being heard. William Seneca, the elected President of the Seneca Nation, said, "It's good to look back and say, 'Well, the white man did this or that to me,' but you also have to look ahead. What we want is a blend of white culture and ours that we can live with, and that will attract our young people back to the reservation."

And at this writing the Indians had been forcibly removed from Alcatraz. They had lived a bleak life there, with Coleman stoves and lanterns for heat and light on the twelve desolate acres of the rock. As their lawyer said, however, Alcatraz did not mean those twelve cold drab acres. It meant "that for the first time in a hundred years, the Indian has stood up for his rights." These Indians were gone, but they were not defeated.

The Indians now seem sure to stand up for their rights. Officially, the federal government seems determined to open a new era for the Indians. Yet progress, and new laws, and new viewpoints are so slow in coming. It is hoped that this book has given a glimpse into the life today of some of the American Indians, and that they will have a better life tomorrow.

SELECTED
BIBLIOGRAPHY

Brophy, William A. and Aberle, Sophie D., compilers, THE INDIAN: AMERICA'S UNFINISHED BUSINESS, Report of the Commission on the Rights, Liberties, and Responsibilities of the American Indian., Norman, Oklahoma, 1966.

Cahn, Edgar S., ed., OUR BROTHER'S KEEPER: THE INDIAN IN WHITE AMERICA, Citizens' Advocate Center, Washington, D.C.: New Community Press, 1969.

Collier, John, INDIANS OF THE AMERICAS, New American Library, New York: Mentor Books, 1961.

Deloria, Jr., Vine, CUSTER DIED FOR YOUR SINS, New York: Macmillan Co. 1969.

————, WE TALK, YOU LISTEN, New York: Macmillan Co., 1970.

Josephy, Jr., Alvin M. THE INDIAN HERITAGE OF AMERICA, New York: Alfred A. Knopf, 1968.

Steiner, Stan, THE NEW INDIANS, New York: Harper & Row, 1968.

NOTE:

Printed source material used in writing this book is too vast to list. Scores of government pamphlets, documents, information sheets, bro-

182

chures, etc., were used. However, significant and outstanding information was contained in the following: several volumes prepared for the Subcommittee on Indian Education of the Committee on Labor and Public Welfare, United States Senate, first session, 91st Congress, printed by the U.S. Government Printing Office, Washington, 1969; printed testimony of the Public Forum before the Committee on Urban Indians in San Francisco, California, of the National Council on Indian Opportunity, April 11–12, 1969; reports, 1965, 1969, of Menominee Indian Study Committee of the Wisconsin Legislative Council; *That These People May Live* by Eileen Maynard and Gayla Twiss, Community Mental Health Program, Pine Ridge Service Unit, Aberdeen Area, Indian Health Service, U.S. Public Health Service, Pine Ridge, South Dakota, 1969; *Assiniboine and Sioux Tribes of the Fort Peck Indian Reservation, Montana*, published by the Fort Peck Agency, Poplar, Montana; *Exclusive Series on South Dakota Indians* by Bill Wagner, originally published in 1968 in the Rapid City (South Dakota) *Journal*, printed by the Office of Economic Opportunity, Washington, D.C.; *The Agua Caliente Indians and Their Guardians,* tribal booklet containing selections from articles and editorials written by George Ringwald, which appeared in the *Press-Enterprise*, Riverside, California; Articles on the Coeur d'Alene Tribe by Oswald C. George, chairman of the Coeur d'Alene Tribal Council, published in the Coeur d'Alene *Press*, Coeur d'Alene, Idaho, 1969, reprinted by the Tribe; *Children of the Sun, A History of the Spokane Indians* by David C. Wynecoop, published by the author, Wellpinit, Washington, 1969; *The Indian Historian*, Winter, 1970, Vol 3, No. 1; *American Indians and the Federal Government*, Bureau of Indian Affairs, U.S. Department of the Interior, Washington, D.C.; *Introducing Modern Medicine in a Navajo Community* by Walsh McDermott, Kurt Deuschle, John Adair, High Fulmer, Bernice Loughlin. Reprint from *Science*, January 22 and 29, 1960. Vol. 131, Nos. 3395 and 3396; *The Medicine Men*, abstracted from paper on "Indian Health Habits and Beliefs," given by Dr. George E. Bock, medical director of the Navajo Indian Health program at a meeting of the Western Surgical Association in Phoenix, Arizona, November, 1966, reprinted from *Public Health Service World*, Vol. 2, No. 4, April, 1967; *Navajo Doctor*, reprinted by the Public Health Service, U.S. Department of Health, Education and Welfare, from *Baylor Medicine*, February, 1967; *A Report on the Programs of the Office of Navajo Economic Opportunity* by Peter MacDonald, Executive Director, July, 1968, Fort Defiance, Arizona; many issues of the *Indian Record*, published monthly by the Department of the Interior, Bureau of Indian Affairs, Washington, D.C.; Office of Navajo Economic Opportunity *Newsletters*; copies of the *Navajo Times*; *Americans Before Columbus* (publication of the National Indian Youth Council); *Alligator Times* (published by the Community Action Program of the Seminole Indians); *Fort Apache Scout*; news articles in *The New York Times*, Washington *Post*, Washington *Evening Star*. Of specific interest were articles in *Time* magazine, July 6, 1970; *The New Republic*, January 17, 1970 ("A Day on Alcatraz"); *The New York Times Magazine*, March 8, 1970 ("This Country Was a Lot Better Off When the Indians Were Running It") by Vine Deloria, Jr.; *The New York Times Magazine*, December 7, 1969 ("The War Between the Redskins and the Feds") by Vine Deloria, Jr.

INDEX

185